50 Taste of Italy Recipes for Home

By: Kelly Johnson

Table of Contents

- Classic Spaghetti Carbonara
- Margherita Pizza
- Osso Buco
- Tiramisu
- Risotto alla Milanese
- Caprese Salad
- Lasagna Bolognese
- Fettuccine Alfredo
- Panzanella
- Eggplant Parmigiana
- Minestrone Soup
- Bruschetta al Pomodoro
- Cannoli Siciliani
- Gnocchi alla Sorrentina
- Ravioli di Ricotta e Spinaci
- Saltimbocca alla Romana
- Panna Cotta
- Arancini
- Pasta e Fagioli
- Insalata Caprese
- Polenta con Funghi
- Zuppa Toscana
- Amatriciana Pasta
- Veal Marsala
- Lemon Sorbetto
- Cioppino
- Cacio e Pepe
- Pistachio Gelato
- Farfalle al Salmone
- Crostini ai Funghi
- Tortellini in Brodo
- Bistecca alla Fiorentina
- Pesto Genovese
- Zeppole di San Giuseppe
- Pasta Primavera
- Sformato di Carciofi

- Pollo alla Cacciatora
- Zabaione
- Insalata di Mare
- Stracciatella Soup
- Tagliatelle al Ragu
- Biscotti di Prato
- Spiedini alla Romana
- Pasta all'Amatriciana
- Polpo alla Griglia
- Sfogliatelle
- Zuppa di Pesce
- Bresaola e Rucola
- Melanzane alla Parmigiana
- Gelato Affogato

Classic Spaghetti Carbonara

Ingredients:

- 8 ounces (225g) spaghetti
- 4 ounces (115g) pancetta or guanciale, diced
- 2 cloves garlic, minced
- 2 large eggs
- 1 cup (100g) grated Pecorino Romano cheese
- Freshly ground black pepper
- Salt (if needed, to taste)
- Fresh parsley, chopped (optional, for garnish)

Instructions:

1. Cook the spaghetti in a large pot of boiling salted water according to package instructions until al dente. Reserve about 1 cup of pasta cooking water, then drain the spaghetti.
2. While the spaghetti is cooking, heat a large skillet over medium heat. Add the diced pancetta or guanciale and cook until crispy and golden brown, about 5-7 minutes. Add the minced garlic and cook for another 1-2 minutes until fragrant. Remove from heat.
3. In a bowl, whisk together the eggs and grated Pecorino Romano cheese until well combined.
4. Quickly toss the hot drained spaghetti in the skillet with the pancetta/guanciale and garlic, ensuring it is well coated with the rendered fat.
5. Remove the skillet from heat and immediately pour the egg and cheese mixture over the pasta, tossing quickly to coat. The heat from the pasta will cook the eggs gently, creating a creamy sauce. If the pasta seems dry, add a bit of the reserved pasta cooking water gradually until desired consistency is reached.
6. Season with freshly ground black pepper to taste. Taste and add salt only if needed, as the pancetta/guanciale and Pecorino Romano are already salty.
7. Serve immediately, garnished with chopped fresh parsley if desired. Enjoy your Classic Spaghetti Carbonara!

Margherita Pizza

Ingredients:

- 1 pizza dough ball (homemade or store-bought)
- 1/2 cup tomato sauce (homemade or good quality store-bought)
- 8 ounces fresh mozzarella cheese, sliced
- Fresh basil leaves
- Extra virgin olive oil
- Salt and freshly ground black pepper

Instructions:

1. **Preheat the oven:** Preheat your oven to the highest temperature it can go, usually around 500-550°F (260-290°C). If you have a pizza stone, place it in the oven during preheating to get it hot.
2. **Prepare the pizza dough:** On a lightly floured surface, stretch or roll out the pizza dough into a round shape of about 12 inches (30 cm) in diameter. Transfer the dough to a pizza peel or a lightly floured cutting board that will fit into your oven.
3. **Assemble the pizza:**
    - Spread the tomato sauce evenly over the pizza dough, leaving a small border around the edges for the crust.
    - Arrange the slices of fresh mozzarella evenly over the sauce.
    - Tear the fresh basil leaves and scatter them over the pizza.
4. **Bake the pizza:** Carefully slide the assembled pizza onto the preheated pizza stone or baking sheet in the oven. Bake for about 8-10 minutes, or until the crust is golden brown and the cheese is bubbly and slightly browned in spots.
5. **Finish and serve:** Remove the pizza from the oven and drizzle lightly with extra virgin olive oil. Season with salt and freshly ground black pepper to taste. Optionally, you can add a few more fresh basil leaves on top for garnish.
6. **Slice and enjoy:** Slice the Margherita Pizza and serve hot. Enjoy the classic flavors of tomato, mozzarella, and basil in this delicious pizza!

This recipe makes one 12-inch Margherita Pizza, perfect for sharing or enjoying on your own!

Osso Buco

Ingredients:

- 4 pieces veal shanks (ossobuco), each about 1.5 inches thick
- Salt and freshly ground black pepper
- All-purpose flour, for dredging
- 4 tablespoons unsalted butter
- 2 tablespoons olive oil
- 1 small onion, finely diced
- 1 small carrot, finely diced
- 1 celery stalk, finely diced
- 3 cloves garlic, minced
- 1 cup dry white wine
- 1 can (14 ounces) diced tomatoes
- 1 cup chicken or beef broth
- 1 bay leaf
- 1 sprig fresh rosemary
- 1 sprig fresh thyme
- Zest of 1 lemon
- Gremolata (optional, for serving):
    - 2 tablespoons chopped fresh parsley
    - 1 clove garlic, minced
    - Zest of 1 lemon

Instructions:

1. **Prepare the veal shanks:** Pat the veal shanks dry with paper towels. Season generously with salt and pepper. Dredge each piece in flour, shaking off any excess.
2. **Brown the veal shanks:** In a large Dutch oven or heavy-bottomed pot, heat 2 tablespoons of butter and 1 tablespoon of olive oil over medium-high heat. Add the veal shanks and brown them on all sides, about 3-4 minutes per side. Work in batches if necessary to avoid overcrowding the pan. Transfer the browned shanks to a plate and set aside.
3. **Prepare the braising liquid:** In the same pot, add the remaining 2 tablespoons of butter and 1 tablespoon of olive oil. Add the diced onion, carrot, celery, and minced garlic. Cook, stirring occasionally, until the vegetables are softened and lightly browned, about 5-7 minutes.
4. **Deglaze the pot:** Pour in the white wine and scrape up any browned bits from the bottom of the pot with a wooden spoon. Let the wine simmer for 2-3 minutes, allowing it to reduce slightly.
5. **Braise the veal shanks:** Return the veal shanks to the pot. Add the diced tomatoes (with their juices), chicken or beef broth, bay leaf, rosemary, thyme, and lemon zest. Bring the liquid to a simmer.

6. **Simmer and braise:** Reduce the heat to low, cover the pot with a lid slightly ajar, and let the osso buco simmer gently for about 2-2.5 hours, or until the meat is very tender and falling off the bone. Stir occasionally and check the liquid level, adding more broth if needed to keep the shanks partially submerged.
7. **Make the gremolata (optional):** In a small bowl, mix together the chopped parsley, minced garlic, and lemon zest. Set aside.
8. **Serve:** Remove the bay leaf, rosemary sprig, and thyme sprig from the pot. Serve the osso buco hot, spooning some of the braising liquid and vegetables over each piece. Garnish with gremolata, if desired.

Osso Buco is traditionally served with risotto Milanese, polenta, or mashed potatoes to soak up the delicious sauce. Enjoy this hearty and flavorful Italian dish!

Tiramisu

Ingredients:

- 6 egg yolks
- 3/4 cup granulated sugar
- 1 cup mascarpone cheese, softened
- 1 1/2 cups heavy cream
- 1 1/2 cups strong brewed coffee or espresso, cooled to room temperature
- 1/4 cup coffee liqueur (optional)
- 2 packages ladyfinger cookies (about 24 cookies)
- Unsweetened cocoa powder, for dusting

Instructions:

1. **Prepare the mascarpone mixture:**
    - In a large mixing bowl, whisk together the egg yolks and sugar until thick and pale in color, about 2-3 minutes.
    - Add the softened mascarpone cheese to the egg yolk mixture and beat until smooth and creamy.
2. **Whip the cream:**
    - In a separate bowl, whip the heavy cream until stiff peaks form.
3. **Combine mascarpone and whipped cream:**
    - Gently fold the whipped cream into the mascarpone mixture until well combined and smooth. Set aside.
4. **Prepare the coffee mixture:**
    - In a shallow dish, combine the cooled brewed coffee or espresso with the coffee liqueur (if using).
5. **Assemble the Tiramisu:**
    - Quickly dip each ladyfinger cookie into the coffee mixture, turning to coat both sides without soaking too much (they should be moistened but not soggy).
    - Arrange a layer of dipped ladyfingers in the bottom of a 9x13-inch (or similar size) dish, breaking them if needed to fit.
    - Spread half of the mascarpone mixture evenly over the ladyfingers.
6. **Repeat layers:**
    - Repeat with another layer of dipped ladyfingers and the remaining mascarpone mixture on top.
7. **Chill and set:**
    - Cover the dish with plastic wrap and refrigerate for at least 4 hours, preferably overnight, to allow the flavors to meld and the tiramisu to set.
8. **Serve:**
    - Before serving, dust the top generously with unsweetened cocoa powder using a fine-mesh sieve.
9. **Enjoy:**

- Cut into squares and serve chilled. Tiramisu is best enjoyed fresh but can be kept refrigerated for up to 2-3 days.

This classic Tiramisu recipe yields a rich and creamy dessert with layers of coffee-soaked ladyfingers and mascarpone cream, topped with a dusting of cocoa powder. It's a perfect treat for any occasion!

Risotto alla Milanese

Ingredients:

- 1 1/2 cups Arborio rice (or other risotto rice)
- 4 cups chicken or vegetable broth, kept warm
- 1/2 cup dry white wine
- 1 small onion, finely chopped
- 2 tablespoons unsalted butter
- 2 tablespoons olive oil
- 1/2 teaspoon saffron threads
- 1/2 cup grated Parmesan cheese
- Salt and freshly ground black pepper, to taste

Instructions:

1. **Prepare the saffron infusion:**
   - In a small bowl, combine the saffron threads with 2 tablespoons of warm water. Let it steep and infuse for about 10-15 minutes.
2. **Start the risotto:**
   - In a large, heavy-bottomed saucepan or skillet, heat 1 tablespoon of butter and 1 tablespoon of olive oil over medium heat.
   - Add the finely chopped onion and sauté until translucent and softened, about 3-4 minutes.
3. **Toast the rice:**
   - Add the Arborio rice to the pan and stir to coat each grain with the butter and oil mixture. Toast the rice for about 2 minutes, stirring frequently, until the edges become translucent.
4. **Deglaze with wine:**
   - Pour in the white wine and stir continuously until the wine is absorbed by the rice.
5. **Add the broth:**
   - Begin adding the warm broth to the rice, one ladleful at a time, stirring constantly and allowing each addition to be absorbed before adding more. This process helps release the starch from the rice, creating a creamy texture. Continue this for about 18-20 minutes, or until the rice is tender but still slightly firm to the bite (al dente).
6. **Incorporate the saffron:**
   - Stir in the saffron infusion, including the saffron threads. This will give the risotto its characteristic yellow color and delicate flavor.
7. **Finish the risotto:**
   - Remove the risotto from heat and stir in the remaining tablespoon of butter and grated Parmesan cheese. Season with salt and freshly ground black pepper to taste. The risotto should be creamy and slightly runny (all'onda).
8. **Serve immediately:**

- Serve the Risotto alla Milanese hot, garnished with additional grated Parmesan cheese if desired.

Risotto alla Milanese is a luxurious and comforting dish that pairs wonderfully with a glass of dry white wine. Enjoy this classic Italian risotto as a main course or alongside grilled meats or seafood.

Caprese Salad

Ingredients:

- 2 large ripe tomatoes, sliced into 1/4-inch thick rounds
- 8 ounces fresh mozzarella cheese, sliced into 1/4-inch thick rounds
- Fresh basil leaves
- Extra virgin olive oil
- Balsamic glaze (optional, for drizzling)
- Salt and freshly ground black pepper, to taste

Instructions:

1. **Prepare the tomatoes and mozzarella:**
   - Slice the tomatoes and fresh mozzarella into rounds that are about 1/4-inch thick. Arrange them alternately on a serving platter or individual plates, overlapping slightly.
2. **Assemble the salad:**
   - Tuck fresh basil leaves between the tomato and mozzarella slices. You can use whole leaves or chiffonade (thinly sliced) basil, depending on your preference.
3. **Season the salad:**
   - Drizzle extra virgin olive oil over the salad, ensuring each slice of tomato and mozzarella gets a bit of oil. Season with salt and freshly ground black pepper to taste.
4. **Optional garnish:**
   - For an extra touch of flavor and presentation, drizzle a small amount of balsamic glaze over the Caprese Salad. The glaze adds a sweet and tangy note that complements the freshness of the tomatoes and basil.
5. **Serve:**
   - Serve the Caprese Salad immediately as a refreshing appetizer or side dish. It's best enjoyed fresh when the flavors of the tomatoes, mozzarella, basil, and olive oil are at their peak.

Caprese Salad is a classic Italian dish that celebrates the flavors of summer with its simplicity and vibrant colors. It's a wonderful addition to any meal and pairs beautifully with crusty bread or as a side to grilled meats or seafood.

Lasagna Bolognese

Ingredients:

For the Bolognese Sauce:

- 1 tablespoon olive oil
- 1 onion, finely chopped
- 2 cloves garlic, minced
- 1 carrot, finely chopped
- 1 celery stalk, finely chopped
- 8 ounces (225g) ground beef
- 8 ounces (225g) ground pork
- 1/2 cup dry red wine
- 1 can (14 ounces/400g) crushed tomatoes
- 1 cup beef or chicken broth
- 1/2 teaspoon dried oregano
- 1/2 teaspoon dried basil
- Salt and freshly ground black pepper, to taste

For the Béchamel Sauce:

- 4 tablespoons unsalted butter
- 1/4 cup all-purpose flour
- 3 cups whole milk
- 1/4 teaspoon ground nutmeg
- Salt and freshly ground black pepper, to taste

For the Lasagna:

- 12 lasagna noodles (oven-ready or cooked according to package instructions)
- 1 1/2 cups shredded mozzarella cheese
- 1/2 cup grated Parmesan cheese
- Fresh basil leaves, for garnish (optional)

Instructions:

1. **Make the Bolognese Sauce:**
   - In a large skillet or saucepan, heat olive oil over medium heat. Add the chopped onion, garlic, carrot, and celery. Sauté until the vegetables are softened, about 5-7 minutes.
   - Add the ground beef and pork to the skillet. Cook, breaking up the meat with a spoon, until browned and cooked through.
   - Pour in the red wine and simmer for a few minutes until most of the liquid evaporates.

- Stir in the crushed tomatoes, beef or chicken broth, dried oregano, dried basil, salt, and pepper. Bring to a simmer, then reduce the heat to low. Cover and simmer gently for 1 to 1.5 hours, stirring occasionally, until the sauce thickens. Adjust seasoning if needed.

2. **Make the Béchamel Sauce:**
   - In a medium saucepan, melt the butter over medium heat. Add the flour and whisk continuously for 1-2 minutes until the mixture is smooth and bubbling.
   - Gradually add the milk, whisking constantly to prevent lumps. Cook the sauce, stirring often, until it thickens enough to coat the back of a spoon, about 5-7 minutes.
   - Stir in the ground nutmeg, salt, and pepper. Remove from heat and set aside.

3. **Assemble the Lasagna:**
   - Preheat your oven to 375°F (190°C).
   - Spread a thin layer of Bolognese sauce on the bottom of a 9x13-inch baking dish.
   - Place a layer of lasagna noodles on top of the sauce, slightly overlapping them.
   - Spread a layer of Béchamel sauce over the noodles, followed by a layer of Bolognese sauce. Sprinkle with shredded mozzarella and grated Parmesan cheese.
   - Repeat the layers: noodles, Béchamel sauce, Bolognese sauce, and cheeses, until you've used all the ingredients, ending with a layer of Bolognese sauce and cheeses on top.

4. **Bake the Lasagna:**
   - Cover the baking dish with aluminum foil, tenting it slightly to prevent the cheese from sticking. Bake in the preheated oven for 30 minutes.
   - Remove the foil and bake for an additional 15 minutes, or until the top is golden brown and bubbly.

5. **Let it rest and serve:**
   - Remove the lasagna from the oven and let it rest for about 10 minutes before slicing.
   - Garnish with fresh basil leaves, if desired, and serve hot.

Lasagna Bolognese is a labor of love but worth every effort with its layers of savory meat sauce, creamy béchamel, and cheesy goodness. Enjoy this classic Italian comfort food with family and friends!

Fettuccine Alfredo

Ingredients:

- 12 ounces (340g) fettuccine pasta
- 1/2 cup unsalted butter
- 1 cup heavy cream
- 1 1/2 cups grated Parmesan cheese, plus extra for serving
- Salt and freshly ground black pepper, to taste
- Fresh parsley, chopped (optional, for garnish)

Instructions:

1. **Cook the pasta:**
   - Bring a large pot of salted water to a boil. Cook the fettuccine according to the package instructions until al dente. Reserve about 1 cup of pasta cooking water, then drain the pasta.
2. **Prepare the sauce:**
   - In a large skillet or saucepan, melt the butter over medium heat.
   - Pour in the heavy cream and bring it to a simmer. Let it cook for about 5 minutes, stirring occasionally, until it slightly thickens.
3. **Add the cheese:**
   - Gradually add the grated Parmesan cheese to the skillet, stirring continuously until the cheese is melted and the sauce is smooth. Season with salt and freshly ground black pepper to taste.
4. **Combine the pasta and sauce:**
   - Add the cooked fettuccine to the skillet with the Alfredo sauce. Toss the pasta gently in the sauce until well coated. If the sauce is too thick, add a little bit of the reserved pasta cooking water at a time to loosen it up.
5. **Serve:**
   - Divide the Fettuccine Alfredo among serving plates or bowls. Garnish with chopped fresh parsley and extra grated Parmesan cheese, if desired.
6. **Enjoy:**
   - Serve immediately while hot and creamy.

Fettuccine Alfredo is best enjoyed freshly made, as the creamy sauce coats the pasta beautifully. It's a comforting and indulgent dish that is sure to satisfy pasta lovers.

Panzanella

Ingredients:

- 4 cups stale bread (preferably Italian or French bread), cut into 1-inch cubes
- 4 large ripe tomatoes, chopped into bite-sized pieces
- 1 cucumber, peeled and sliced
- 1/2 red onion, thinly sliced
- 1 bell pepper (red, yellow, or green), seeded and chopped
- 1/4 cup fresh basil leaves, torn or chopped
- 1/4 cup fresh parsley leaves, chopped
- 1/2 cup Kalamata olives, pitted and halved (optional)
- 1/3 cup extra virgin olive oil
- 3 tablespoons red wine vinegar or balsamic vinegar
- Salt and freshly ground black pepper, to taste

Instructions:

1. **Prepare the bread:**
   - If your bread isn't already stale, you can toast the bread cubes in a preheated oven at 350°F (175°C) for about 10 minutes, or until they are golden and crisp. Set aside to cool.
2. **Assemble the salad:**
   - In a large mixing bowl, combine the chopped tomatoes, sliced cucumber, thinly sliced red onion, chopped bell pepper, torn basil leaves, chopped parsley, and Kalamata olives (if using).
3. **Make the dressing:**
   - In a small bowl or jar, whisk together the extra virgin olive oil and red wine vinegar or balsamic vinegar. Season with salt and freshly ground black pepper to taste.
4. **Combine everything:**
   - Add the toasted bread cubes to the bowl of vegetables and herbs.
   - Pour the dressing over the salad and toss gently to combine, ensuring all ingredients are coated evenly with the dressing. Allow the salad to sit for about 10-15 minutes before serving, so the bread can absorb some of the flavors.
5. **Serve:**
   - Serve the Panzanella salad immediately at room temperature, allowing the flavors to meld together. It's perfect as a side dish or a light main course on a warm summer day.

Panzanella is a delightful way to use up stale bread and celebrate the bounty of fresh vegetables and herbs. It's colorful, flavorful, and brings a taste of Italy to your table!

Eggplant Parmigiana

Ingredients:

- 2 large eggplants, sliced into 1/2-inch rounds
- Salt, for sprinkling
- 1 cup all-purpose flour
- 3 large eggs, beaten
- 2 cups breadcrumbs (preferably seasoned)
- Vegetable oil, for frying
- 2 cups marinara sauce or tomato sauce
- 1 cup grated Parmesan cheese
- 1 cup shredded mozzarella cheese
- Fresh basil leaves, chopped (optional, for garnish)

Instructions:

1. **Prepare the eggplant:**
    - Place the eggplant slices on a baking sheet and sprinkle both sides generously with salt. Let them sit for about 30 minutes to draw out bitterness. Pat dry with paper towels.
2. **Coat and fry the eggplant:**
    - Set up three shallow dishes: one with flour, one with beaten eggs, and one with breadcrumbs.
    - Dredge each eggplant slice in flour, shaking off excess, then dip into the beaten eggs, and finally coat evenly with breadcrumbs, pressing gently to adhere.
    - In a large skillet, heat about 1/2 inch of vegetable oil over medium-high heat. Fry the eggplant slices in batches until golden brown and crispy on both sides, about 2-3 minutes per side. Transfer to a plate lined with paper towels to drain excess oil.
3. **Assemble the Eggplant Parmigiana:**
    - Preheat your oven to 375°F (190°C). Lightly grease a 9x13-inch baking dish.
    - Spread a thin layer of marinara or tomato sauce on the bottom of the baking dish.
    - Arrange a layer of fried eggplant slices over the sauce, slightly overlapping them if needed.
    - Spoon more sauce over the eggplant slices, then sprinkle with grated Parmesan cheese and shredded mozzarella cheese.
    - Repeat layers: eggplant slices, sauce, Parmesan cheese, and mozzarella cheese, until you've used all the ingredients, finishing with a layer of sauce and cheeses on top.
4. **Bake the Eggplant Parmigiana:**
    - Cover the baking dish with aluminum foil and bake in the preheated oven for 30 minutes.
    - Remove the foil and bake for an additional 10-15 minutes, or until the cheese is melted and bubbly and the sauce is hot and bubbly.

5. **Serve:**
    - Remove the Eggplant Parmigiana from the oven and let it cool slightly before serving. Garnish with chopped fresh basil leaves, if desired.

Eggplant Parmigiana is delicious served hot, straight from the oven. It makes a satisfying main dish alongside a green salad or crusty bread, bringing the flavors of Italy to your table. Enjoy this comforting and cheesy classic!

Minestrone Soup

Ingredients:

- 2 tablespoons olive oil
- 1 onion, diced
- 2 cloves garlic, minced
- 2 carrots, diced
- 2 celery stalks, diced
- 1 zucchini, diced
- 1 yellow squash, diced
- 1 cup green beans, trimmed and cut into bite-sized pieces
- 1 can (14 ounces) diced tomatoes (or 2 cups fresh tomatoes, diced)
- 6 cups vegetable or chicken broth
- 1 teaspoon dried oregano
- 1 teaspoon dried basil
- 1 teaspoon dried thyme
- Salt and freshly ground black pepper, to taste
- 1 can (15 ounces) cannellini beans, drained and rinsed (or any other beans of your choice)
- 1 cup small pasta (such as ditalini, elbow macaroni, or small shells)
- Fresh parsley, chopped, for garnish
- Grated Parmesan cheese, for serving (optional)

Instructions:

1. **Sauté aromatics:**
    - In a large pot or Dutch oven, heat olive oil over medium heat. Add the diced onion and cook until translucent, about 5 minutes. Add minced garlic and cook for another 1-2 minutes until fragrant.
2. **Add vegetables:**
    - Add diced carrots, celery, zucchini, yellow squash, and green beans to the pot. Cook for about 5-7 minutes, stirring occasionally, until the vegetables start to soften.
3. **Simmer with tomatoes and broth:**
    - Stir in the diced tomatoes (with their juices) and vegetable or chicken broth. Add dried oregano, basil, thyme, salt, and pepper to taste. Bring the soup to a boil, then reduce the heat to low. Cover and let it simmer for about 15-20 minutes, or until the vegetables are tender.
4. **Add beans and pasta:**
    - Add the drained and rinsed cannellini beans to the soup. Also, add the small pasta (ditalini, elbow macaroni, or small shells). Continue to simmer for another 10-12 minutes, or until the pasta is cooked al dente.
5. **Adjust seasoning and serve:**

- Taste and adjust the seasoning with more salt and pepper if needed. Stir in chopped fresh parsley just before serving.
6. **Serve hot:**
    - Ladle the Minestrone Soup into bowls. Optionally, sprinkle with grated Parmesan cheese on top before serving.

Minestrone Soup is best enjoyed hot and fresh, accompanied by crusty bread or a side salad. It's a comforting and nutritious dish that's perfect for cooler weather or any time you crave a hearty soup!

Bruschetta al Pomodoro

Ingredients:

- 4-5 ripe tomatoes, diced
- 2 cloves garlic, minced
- 6-8 fresh basil leaves, chopped
- 2 tablespoons extra virgin olive oil, plus extra for drizzling
- 1 teaspoon balsamic vinegar (optional)
- Salt and freshly ground black pepper, to taste
- 1 loaf of Italian bread or baguette, sliced into 1/2-inch thick slices
- 1-2 tablespoons olive oil, for brushing the bread

Instructions:

1. **Prepare the tomato topping:**
    - In a mixing bowl, combine the diced tomatoes, minced garlic, chopped basil leaves, extra virgin olive oil, and balsamic vinegar (if using). Season with salt and pepper to taste. Toss gently to combine all the ingredients. Let the mixture marinate at room temperature while you prepare the bread.
2. **Toast the bread:**
    - Preheat your grill, grill pan, or oven broiler.
    - Brush both sides of each bread slice with olive oil. Grill or toast the bread slices until golden brown and crisp on both sides. If using a grill or grill pan, it usually takes about 1-2 minutes per side. If using the oven broiler, place the bread slices on a baking sheet and broil for about 2-3 minutes per side, watching closely to prevent burning.
3. **Assemble the bruschetta:**
    - Arrange the toasted bread slices on a serving platter or plate.
    - Spoon the tomato mixture generously over each slice of bread, allowing some of the juices to soak into the bread.
    - Drizzle a little extra virgin olive oil over the top of each bruschetta for added flavor and shine.
4. **Serve immediately:**
    - Serve the Bruschetta al Pomodoro immediately as an appetizer or snack. Enjoy the fresh flavors of tomatoes, garlic, and basil with the crispy toast.

Bruschetta al Pomodoro is a delightful dish that captures the essence of Italian cuisine with its simple yet vibrant ingredients. It's perfect for entertaining guests or as a light starter before a meal. Buon appetito!

Cannoli Siciliani

Ingredients:

For the Cannoli Shells:

- 2 cups all-purpose flour
- 2 tablespoons granulated sugar
- 1/4 teaspoon salt
- 2 tablespoons unsalted butter, softened
- 1 egg yolk
- 1/2 cup Marsala wine (or dry white wine)
- Vegetable oil, for frying
- Cannoli tubes or metal cannoli forms

For the Filling:

- 2 cups whole milk ricotta cheese, drained
- 3/4 cup powdered sugar, sifted
- 1/2 teaspoon vanilla extract
- 1/4 cup finely chopped candied citron or orange zest (optional)
- Powdered sugar, for dusting

Optional Garnish:

- Finely chopped pistachios
- Chocolate chips
- Candied fruit

Instructions:

1. **Make the Cannoli Shells:**
   - In a large bowl, whisk together the flour, granulated sugar, and salt.
   - Add the softened butter and egg yolk to the dry ingredients. Mix together until crumbly.
   - Gradually add the Marsala wine, mixing with a fork or your hands until the dough comes together into a smooth ball.
   - On a lightly floured surface, knead the dough for about 5 minutes until it's elastic and smooth.
   - Wrap the dough in plastic wrap and let it rest at room temperature for at least 30 minutes.
2. **Roll and Fry the Cannoli Shells:**
   - Divide the dough into two portions. Keep one portion covered while you work with the other.
   - Roll out the dough very thinly on a lightly floured surface or using a pasta machine, until it's about 1/8 inch thick.

- Use a round cookie cutter or a glass to cut out circles of dough about 4-5 inches in diameter.
- Wrap each circle of dough around a cannoli tube or metal form, sealing the edges with a little water.
- Heat vegetable oil in a deep fryer or large pot to 350°F (175°C).
- Fry the cannoli shells in batches until golden brown and crispy, about 2-3 minutes. Use tongs to carefully remove them from the oil and place them on paper towels to drain and cool.
- Once cooled, gently slide the shells off the cannoli tubes or forms. Let them cool completely before filling.

3. **Make the Filling:**
    - In a mixing bowl, combine the drained ricotta cheese, powdered sugar, and vanilla extract. Mix until smooth and creamy.
    - Stir in the chopped candied citron or orange zest, if using, for added flavor.
    - Cover the filling and refrigerate for at least 30 minutes to firm up.

4. **Assemble the Cannoli:**
    - Fill a piping bag fitted with a large star tip (or use a spoon) with the chilled ricotta filling.
    - Pipe the filling into each end of the cannoli shells, starting from the center and filling towards the ends. Alternatively, you can dip the ends of the shells into the filling.
    - Optional: Dip the ends of each cannoli into finely chopped pistachios, chocolate chips, or press pieces of candied fruit onto the ends.
    - Dust the filled cannoli with powdered sugar just before serving.

5. **Serve and Enjoy:**
    - Cannoli Siciliani are best served fresh. Enjoy these delicious Italian pastries as a delightful dessert or treat. They pair wonderfully with a cup of espresso or a sweet dessert wine.

Cannoli Siciliani are a labor of love but worth the effort for their crispy shells and creamy, sweet filling. They're a beloved dessert that's sure to impress at any gathering or special occasion. Buon appetito!

Gnocchi alla Sorrentina

Ingredients:

- 1 pound (about 500g) potato gnocchi (store-bought or homemade)
- 2 cups marinara sauce or tomato passata
- 1 cup shredded mozzarella cheese
- 1/2 cup grated Parmesan cheese
- Fresh basil leaves, torn, for garnish
- Salt and freshly ground black pepper, to taste
- Olive oil, for drizzling

Instructions:

1. **Preheat the Oven:**
   - Preheat your oven to 375°F (190°C). Grease a baking dish with olive oil or cooking spray.
2. **Cook the Gnocchi:**
   - Bring a large pot of salted water to a boil. Cook the gnocchi according to the package instructions or until they float to the surface, indicating they're cooked. Drain well.
3. **Assemble the Dish:**
   - Spread a thin layer of marinara sauce on the bottom of the prepared baking dish.
   - Arrange half of the cooked gnocchi in a single layer over the sauce.
   - Spoon half of the remaining marinara sauce over the gnocchi, spreading it evenly.
   - Sprinkle half of the shredded mozzarella and grated Parmesan cheese over the sauce.
   - Season lightly with salt and freshly ground black pepper.
4. **Repeat the Layers:**
   - Add the remaining half of the cooked gnocchi in another layer on top.
   - Pour the rest of the marinara sauce over the gnocchi.
   - Sprinkle the remaining shredded mozzarella and grated Parmesan cheese on top.
5. **Bake the Gnocchi alla Sorrentina:**
   - Cover the baking dish with aluminum foil and bake in the preheated oven for 20 minutes.
   - Remove the foil and bake for an additional 10 minutes, or until the cheese is melted and bubbly and the gnocchi are heated through.
6. **Serve:**
   - Remove the Gnocchi alla Sorrentina from the oven and let it cool slightly.
   - Garnish with torn fresh basil leaves and drizzle with a little olive oil.
   - Serve hot, portioned onto plates, and enjoy this comforting Italian dish!

Gnocchi alla Sorrentina is a delicious and satisfying meal that combines the pillowy texture of gnocchi with the richness of tomato sauce and melted cheese. It's perfect for a cozy dinner at home with family or friends. Buon appetito!

Ravioli di Ricotta e Spinaci

Ingredients:

For the Ravioli Dough:

- 2 cups all-purpose flour, plus extra for dusting
- 2 large eggs
- 1/4 teaspoon salt
- 1-2 tablespoons water, if needed

For the Filling:

- 1 cup ricotta cheese, drained if necessary
- 1 cup cooked spinach, squeezed dry and finely chopped
- 1/2 cup grated Parmesan cheese
- 1 egg yolk
- 1/4 teaspoon ground nutmeg
- Salt and freshly ground black pepper, to taste

For Serving:

- Marinara sauce or sage butter sauce
- Grated Parmesan cheese, for garnish
- Fresh basil or parsley, chopped, for garnish (optional)

Instructions:

1. **Make the Ravioli Dough:**
   - On a clean work surface, mound the flour and make a well in the center.
   - Crack the eggs into the well and add salt.
   - Using a fork, gradually whisk the eggs, incorporating flour from the sides of the well.
   - Once the dough starts to come together, knead it with your hands until smooth and elastic, adding water if the dough is too dry or more flour if it's too sticky.
   - Wrap the dough in plastic wrap and let it rest at room temperature for at least 30 minutes.
2. **Prepare the Filling:**
   - In a mixing bowl, combine the drained ricotta cheese, chopped cooked spinach, grated Parmesan cheese, egg yolk, ground nutmeg, salt, and pepper. Mix well until all ingredients are evenly incorporated. Adjust seasoning to taste.
3. **Assemble the Ravioli:**
   - Divide the rested dough into smaller portions and roll out each portion thinly using a pasta machine or rolling pin, dusting with flour as needed to prevent sticking.

- Place teaspoonfuls of the ricotta and spinach filling on one sheet of dough, leaving space between each mound of filling.
- Brush the edges of the dough with water to help seal the ravioli.
- Place another sheet of dough over the filling and press down around each mound of filling to seal, pressing out any air pockets.
- Use a ravioli cutter or a knife to cut out individual ravioli squares or circles. Press the edges with a fork to ensure they are sealed.

4. **Cook the Ravioli:**
    - Bring a large pot of salted water to a boil.
    - Carefully drop the ravioli into the boiling water, working in batches if necessary to avoid overcrowding.
    - Cook the ravioli for about 3-4 minutes, or until they float to the surface and are cooked through.

5. **Serve:**
    - Remove the cooked ravioli with a slotted spoon and place them on serving plates.
    - Spoon marinara sauce or sage butter sauce over the ravioli.
    - Garnish with grated Parmesan cheese and chopped fresh basil or parsley, if desired.
    - Serve immediately and enjoy your homemade Ravioli di Ricotta e Spinaci!

This dish is a labor of love but well worth the effort for its delicate flavors and satisfying texture. It's perfect for a special occasion or when you want to impress with homemade Italian cuisine. Buon appetito!

Saltimbocca alla Romana

Ingredients:

- 4 veal scallops (about 4-6 ounces each), pounded thin
- 4 slices prosciutto di Parma (thinly sliced)
- 8 fresh sage leaves
- All-purpose flour, for dredging
- Salt and freshly ground black pepper, to taste
- 1/4 cup unsalted butter
- 1/2 cup dry white wine
- 1/4 cup chicken broth or beef broth (optional)
- 1 lemon, sliced (for garnish)

Instructions:

1. **Prepare the Veal:**
   - Season the veal scallops with salt and pepper on both sides.
   - Place a slice of prosciutto on each veal scallop, covering the meat.
   - Secure the prosciutto and sage leaves to the veal scallops with toothpicks, threading through the sage leaves.
2. **Dredge and Cook:**
   - Dredge the veal scallops in flour, shaking off any excess.
   - In a large skillet, melt the butter over medium-high heat.
   - Once the butter is hot and foamy, add the veal scallops to the skillet, prosciutto-side down.
   - Cook for about 2-3 minutes on each side, or until the veal is golden brown and cooked through. Transfer the cooked veal scallops to a plate and cover loosely with foil to keep warm.
3. **Deglaze the Pan:**
   - Pour the white wine into the skillet, stirring and scraping up any browned bits from the bottom of the pan with a wooden spoon.
   - Add the chicken or beef broth (if using) and continue to cook for another 2-3 minutes, allowing the sauce to reduce slightly.
4. **Serve:**
   - Arrange the veal scallops on serving plates.
   - Spoon the pan sauce over the veal scallops.
   - Garnish with lemon slices and additional fresh sage leaves, if desired.
   - Serve immediately, accompanied by your choice of side dishes like roasted potatoes or a simple green salad.

Saltimbocca alla Romana is a flavorful dish with a perfect balance of salty prosciutto, aromatic sage, and tangy white wine sauce. It's a classic Italian recipe that is sure to impress at any dinner table. Buon appetito!

Panna Cotta

Ingredients:

- 2 cups heavy cream
- 1/2 cup whole milk
- 1/2 cup granulated sugar
- 1 vanilla bean or 1 teaspoon vanilla extract
- 2 1/4 teaspoons powdered gelatin (or 1 packet, about 7g)
- 3 tablespoons cold water

Optional Toppings:

- Fresh berries (strawberries, raspberries, blueberries)
- Fruit coulis (strawberry, raspberry, mango)
- Chocolate sauce
- Caramel sauce
- Mint leaves, for garnish

Instructions:

1. **Prepare the Gelatin:**
    - In a small bowl, sprinkle the powdered gelatin over the cold water. Let it sit for about 5-10 minutes to soften.
2. **Prepare the Panna Cotta Mixture:**
    - In a saucepan, combine the heavy cream, whole milk, and granulated sugar.
    - If using a vanilla bean, split it lengthwise and scrape the seeds into the cream mixture. Add the vanilla bean pod as well. If using vanilla extract, add it after heating the cream mixture.
    - Heat the mixture over medium heat, stirring occasionally, until it reaches a simmer. Do not boil.
3. **Dissolve the Gelatin:**
    - Remove the cream mixture from heat. Remove the vanilla bean pod if using.
    - Add the softened gelatin to the hot cream mixture, stirring until completely dissolved.
4. **Cool and Pour:**
    - Let the mixture cool slightly for about 5-10 minutes.
    - Pour the mixture into individual serving dishes or molds. You can use ramekins, glasses, or silicone molds for different shapes.
5. **Chill and Set:**
    - Cover each dish or mold with plastic wrap to prevent a skin from forming.
    - Refrigerate the Panna Cotta for at least 4 hours, or until set firm. For best results, refrigerate overnight.
6. **Serve:**

- To serve, carefully unmold the Panna Cotta onto serving plates, if desired. If using ramekins or glasses, you can serve directly in them.
- Garnish with fresh berries, fruit coulis, chocolate sauce, caramel sauce, or mint leaves, as desired.

7. **Enjoy:**
   - Panna Cotta is best served chilled. It's a luxurious and creamy dessert that melts in your mouth, perfect for any occasion.

This recipe makes about 4 servings of Panna Cotta. It's a versatile dessert that can be customized with various toppings to suit your preference. Enjoy this Italian classic with friends and family!

Arancini

Ingredients:

For the Risotto:

- 1 cup Arborio rice (or other short-grain rice suitable for risotto)
- 3 cups chicken or vegetable broth
- 1/2 cup dry white wine (optional)
- 1/2 cup grated Parmesan cheese
- 2 tablespoons unsalted butter
- Salt and freshly ground black pepper, to taste

For the Filling:

- 1 cup ragù sauce (meat sauce) or marinara sauce
- 1/2 cup mozzarella cheese, diced into small cubes
- 1/4 cup grated Parmesan cheese

For Coating and Frying:

- 2 cups plain breadcrumbs
- 2 large eggs, beaten
- Vegetable oil, for frying

Optional:

- Fresh parsley, chopped (for garnish)
- Marinara sauce (for dipping)

Instructions:

1. **Prepare the Risotto:**
   - In a saucepan, bring the chicken or vegetable broth to a simmer over medium heat. Keep it warm while you prepare the risotto.
   - In a separate large saucepan or skillet, melt 1 tablespoon of butter over medium heat. Add the Arborio rice and toast it for 1-2 minutes, stirring constantly.
   - Pour in the white wine (if using) and cook until it has evaporated.
   - Begin adding the warm broth to the rice, one ladleful at a time, stirring frequently. Allow each addition of broth to be absorbed before adding more. Continue this process until the rice is creamy and tender, about 20-25 minutes.
   - Stir in the grated Parmesan cheese and remaining butter. Season with salt and pepper to taste. Spread the risotto onto a large baking sheet to cool completely.
2. **Form and Fill the Arancini:**
   - Once the risotto has cooled, take a handful of risotto and flatten it in your hand.

- Place a spoonful of ragù or marinara sauce and a cube of mozzarella cheese in the center of the flattened risotto.
- Enclose the filling by shaping the risotto into a ball, about the size of a golf ball. Ensure the filling is completely sealed within the rice ball.

3. **Coat and Fry the Arancini:**
    - Prepare two shallow dishes: one with beaten eggs and another with breadcrumbs.
    - Dip each rice ball into the beaten eggs, ensuring it is fully coated.
    - Roll the coated rice ball in the breadcrumbs, pressing gently to adhere.
    - In a large skillet or deep fryer, heat vegetable oil to 350°F (175°C). Fry the arancini in batches until golden brown and crispy, about 3-4 minutes per batch. Transfer to a plate lined with paper towels to drain excess oil.

4. **Serve:**
    - Serve the arancini hot, garnished with chopped parsley if desired.
    - Optionally, serve with marinara sauce for dipping.

Arancini are best enjoyed fresh and hot, with the creamy risotto center and flavorful filling. They make a delicious appetizer or snack that will impress your guests with their crunchy exterior and gooey interior. Buon appetito!

Pasta e Fagioli

Ingredients:

- 1 tablespoon olive oil
- 1 onion, finely chopped
- 2 cloves garlic, minced
- 2 carrots, diced
- 2 celery stalks, diced
- 1 can (15 ounces) cannellini beans, drained and rinsed (or 1 1/2 cups cooked cannellini beans)
- 1 can (15 ounces) diced tomatoes
- 4 cups vegetable or chicken broth
- 1 teaspoon dried oregano
- 1 teaspoon dried basil
- 1/2 teaspoon dried thyme
- Salt and freshly ground black pepper, to taste
- 1 cup small pasta (such as ditalini, elbow macaroni, or small shells)
- Fresh parsley, chopped, for garnish
- Grated Parmesan cheese, for serving (optional)

Instructions:

1. **Sauté Vegetables:**
   - Heat olive oil in a large pot or Dutch oven over medium heat. Add chopped onion, garlic, carrots, and celery. Sauté for 5-7 minutes, or until vegetables are softened.
2. **Add Beans and Tomatoes:**
   - Add cannellini beans and diced tomatoes (with their juices) to the pot. Stir to combine.
3. **Simmer Soup:**
   - Pour in vegetable or chicken broth. Add dried oregano, basil, thyme, salt, and pepper to taste. Bring the soup to a boil, then reduce heat to low. Cover and let it simmer for about 15-20 minutes to allow the flavors to meld together.
4. **Cook Pasta:**
   - Meanwhile, cook the small pasta according to the package instructions in a separate pot of salted boiling water until al dente. Drain and set aside.
5. **Combine Pasta and Soup:**
   - Add the cooked pasta to the soup pot. Stir well to combine. If the soup is too thick, you can add a bit more broth or water to reach your desired consistency.
6. **Serve:**
   - Ladle Pasta e Fagioli into bowls. Garnish with chopped fresh parsley and grated Parmesan cheese, if desired.
   - Serve hot, accompanied by crusty bread or a side salad.

Pasta e Fagioli is a comforting and nutritious soup that is perfect for colder days. It's simple to prepare yet full of hearty flavors from the beans, vegetables, and aromatic herbs. Enjoy this classic Italian dish with your family and friends!

Insalata Caprese

Ingredients:

- 3-4 ripe tomatoes, sliced into 1/4-inch thick rounds
- 1 pound fresh mozzarella cheese, sliced into 1/4-inch thick rounds
- Fresh basil leaves
- Extra virgin olive oil, for drizzling
- Balsamic glaze or balsamic vinegar (optional)
- Salt and freshly ground black pepper, to taste

Instructions:

1. **Assemble the Salad:**
    - Arrange alternating slices of tomatoes and mozzarella cheese on a serving platter or individual plates.
    - Tuck fresh basil leaves between the tomato and mozzarella slices.
2. **Season:**
    - Season the salad with salt and freshly ground black pepper to taste.
3. **Drizzle:**
    - Drizzle extra virgin olive oil over the salad. For added flavor, you can also drizzle a balsamic glaze or balsamic vinegar over the top.
4. **Serve:**
    - Serve the Insalata Caprese immediately, while the ingredients are fresh and vibrant.

Insalata Caprese is a light and elegant dish that highlights the flavors of fresh tomatoes, creamy mozzarella, and aromatic basil. It's perfect as an appetizer, side dish, or even a light lunch during the summer months when tomatoes are at their peak. Enjoy this classic Italian salad with a glass of crisp white wine for a true taste of Italy!

Polenta con Funghi

Ingredients:

For the Polenta:

- 1 cup polenta (cornmeal)
- 4 cups water
- 1 teaspoon salt
- 2 tablespoons unsalted butter
- 1/2 cup grated Parmesan cheese

For the Mushroom Sauce:

- 1 pound mixed mushrooms (such as cremini, shiitake, and oyster), sliced
- 2 cloves garlic, minced
- 1 small onion, finely chopped
- 2 tablespoons olive oil
- 1/2 cup dry white wine
- 1/2 cup vegetable or chicken broth
- 1/2 cup heavy cream
- Salt and freshly ground black pepper, to taste
- Fresh parsley, chopped, for garnish
- Grated Parmesan cheese, for serving (optional)

Instructions:

1. **Prepare the Polenta:**
    - In a large saucepan, bring 4 cups of water to a boil.
    - Gradually whisk in the polenta and salt, stirring constantly to prevent lumps.
    - Reduce the heat to low and cook the polenta, stirring frequently, for about 20-25 minutes or until thickened and creamy.
    - Stir in the butter and grated Parmesan cheese until well combined. Adjust seasoning if needed. Cover and keep warm.
2. **Make the Mushroom Sauce:**
    - In a large skillet, heat olive oil over medium heat. Add minced garlic and chopped onion. Sauté for 2-3 minutes until fragrant and softened.
    - Add sliced mushrooms to the skillet. Cook, stirring occasionally, until the mushrooms are golden brown and softened, about 5-7 minutes.
    - Pour in the white wine and cook for another 2-3 minutes, allowing the alcohol to evaporate.
    - Stir in the vegetable or chicken broth and bring to a simmer. Cook for 5 minutes until slightly reduced.

- Add the heavy cream to the skillet, stirring gently to combine. Simmer for another 2-3 minutes until the sauce thickens slightly. Season with salt and pepper to taste.
3. **Serve:**
    - Spoon the creamy polenta onto serving plates or bowls.
    - Top with a generous amount of mushroom sauce.
    - Garnish with chopped fresh parsley and grated Parmesan cheese, if desired.
    - Serve immediately while hot.

Polenta con Funghi is a comforting and flavorful dish that combines the creamy texture of polenta with the earthy richness of mushroom sauce. It makes a satisfying main course or a hearty side dish for any occasion. Enjoy this classic Italian dish with a glass of red wine for a delightful meal!

Zuppa Toscana

Ingredients:

- 1 pound Italian sausage (mild or spicy), casings removed
- 1 large onion, diced
- 3 cloves garlic, minced
- 4 cups chicken broth
- 2 cups water
- 3 large potatoes, peeled and diced into bite-sized pieces
- 1 bunch kale, tough stems removed and leaves chopped
- 1 cup heavy cream
- Salt and freshly ground black pepper, to taste
- Grated Parmesan cheese, for serving (optional)
- Red pepper flakes, for serving (optional)

Instructions:

1. **Cook the Italian Sausage:**
   - In a large pot or Dutch oven, cook the Italian sausage over medium-high heat, breaking it into small pieces with a spoon or spatula. Cook until browned and cooked through, about 5-7 minutes.
   - Remove the cooked sausage from the pot and set it aside on a plate lined with paper towels to drain excess fat.
2. **Sauté Onion and Garlic:**
   - In the same pot, add diced onion. Sauté for 3-4 minutes until softened and translucent.
   - Add minced garlic and cook for an additional 1-2 minutes until fragrant.
3. **Simmer Soup:**
   - Pour in chicken broth and water. Stir well, scraping up any browned bits from the bottom of the pot.
   - Add diced potatoes to the pot. Bring the mixture to a boil, then reduce heat to medium-low. Simmer uncovered for about 10-15 minutes, or until the potatoes are tender when pierced with a fork.
4. **Add Kale and Cream:**
   - Stir in chopped kale leaves and cooked Italian sausage. Simmer for another 5 minutes, allowing the kale to wilt and soften.
   - Pour in heavy cream, stirring gently to combine. Cook for an additional 2-3 minutes until heated through.
   - Season with salt and freshly ground black pepper to taste.
5. **Serve:**
   - Ladle Zuppa Toscana into bowls. Sprinkle with grated Parmesan cheese and red pepper flakes, if desired.
   - Serve hot, accompanied by crusty bread for dipping.

Zuppa Toscana is a comforting and satisfying soup that combines the richness of sausage and cream with the heartiness of potatoes and kale. It's perfect for chilly days and makes a complete meal on its own. Enjoy this classic Italian soup with friends and family!

Amatriciana Pasta

Ingredients:

- 1/4 pound (about 100g) guanciale or pancetta, diced
- 1 tablespoon olive oil
- 1 small onion, finely chopped
- 2 cloves garlic, minced
- 1/4 teaspoon red pepper flakes (adjust to taste)
- 1 can (14 ounces) crushed tomatoes
- Salt and freshly ground black pepper, to taste
- 1 pound (about 450g) bucatini pasta (or spaghetti)
- 1/2 cup grated Pecorino Romano cheese, plus extra for serving
- Fresh parsley or basil, chopped (optional, for garnish)

Instructions:

1. **Cook the Guanciale:**
    - Heat olive oil in a large skillet over medium heat. Add the diced guanciale (or pancetta) and cook until it becomes crispy and golden brown, about 5-7 minutes. Remove from the skillet and place on a paper towel-lined plate to drain excess fat. Set aside.
2. **Prepare the Sauce:**
    - In the same skillet with the rendered fat from the guanciale, add the chopped onion. Sauté for about 3-4 minutes until softened and translucent.
    - Add minced garlic and red pepper flakes. Cook for another 1-2 minutes until fragrant.
3. **Simmer the Tomato Sauce:**
    - Pour in the crushed tomatoes, stirring to combine. Season with salt and freshly ground black pepper to taste.
    - Bring the sauce to a simmer, then reduce the heat to low. Let it simmer gently for about 15-20 minutes, stirring occasionally, until the sauce thickens slightly.
4. **Cook the Pasta:**
    - While the sauce is simmering, cook the bucatini pasta in a large pot of salted boiling water according to the package instructions until al dente. Reserve about 1 cup of pasta cooking water before draining.
5. **Combine Sauce and Pasta:**
    - Add the cooked guanciale (or pancetta) back into the skillet with the tomato sauce. Stir to combine and let it simmer together for another minute.
    - Add the drained bucatini pasta directly to the skillet with the sauce. Toss well to coat the pasta evenly with the sauce, adding a splash of reserved pasta cooking water if needed to loosen the sauce.
6. **Finish and Serve:**
    - Remove the skillet from heat and sprinkle grated Pecorino Romano cheese over the pasta. Toss again to combine.

- Divide the Amatriciana pasta among serving plates or bowls. Garnish with additional Pecorino Romano cheese and chopped parsley or basil, if desired.
- Serve immediately while hot, and enjoy this delicious and flavorful Italian pasta dish!

Amatriciana pasta is a savory and satisfying dish that celebrates the bold flavors of Italian cuisine. It's perfect for pasta lovers and can be enjoyed as a main course for a comforting meal. Buon appetito!

Veal Marsala

Ingredients:

- 4 veal cutlets, pounded to about 1/4-inch thickness
- Salt and freshly ground black pepper, to taste
- All-purpose flour, for dredging
- 4 tablespoons unsalted butter, divided
- 2 tablespoons olive oil
- 1/2 cup Marsala wine
- 1/2 cup chicken broth
- 1/2 cup heavy cream (optional)
- Fresh parsley, chopped, for garnish

Instructions:

1. **Prepare the Veal Cutlets:**
    - Season the veal cutlets with salt and pepper on both sides.
    - Dredge each cutlet in flour, shaking off any excess.
2. **Cook the Veal Cutlets:**
    - In a large skillet, heat 2 tablespoons of butter and 1 tablespoon of olive oil over medium-high heat.
    - Add the veal cutlets to the skillet (you may need to do this in batches to avoid overcrowding the pan). Cook for about 2-3 minutes per side, or until golden brown and cooked through.
    - Transfer the cooked veal cutlets to a plate and cover loosely with foil to keep warm.
3. **Make the Marsala Sauce:**
    - In the same skillet, add the remaining 2 tablespoons of butter and 1 tablespoon of olive oil.
    - Add Marsala wine to the skillet, scraping up any browned bits from the bottom of the pan with a wooden spoon.
    - Cook for about 2 minutes, allowing the Marsala wine to reduce slightly.
    - Stir in chicken broth and bring the mixture to a simmer. Cook for another 2-3 minutes until the sauce thickens slightly.
4. **Finish the Dish:**
    - Optional: If using heavy cream, reduce the heat to low and stir in the cream. Simmer gently for 1-2 minutes until the sauce is creamy and heated through.
    - Return the veal cutlets to the skillet, turning them to coat evenly with the sauce. Let them simmer in the sauce for a minute or two to absorb flavors.
5. **Serve:**
    - Transfer the veal cutlets to serving plates.
    - Spoon the Marsala sauce over the veal cutlets.
    - Garnish with chopped fresh parsley.

- Serve immediately, accompanied by your choice of side dishes like mashed potatoes, pasta, or vegetables.

Veal Marsala is a luxurious dish with tender veal and a rich, flavorful sauce that is perfect for special occasions or when you want to impress with Italian cuisine. Enjoy this delicious dish with a glass of Marsala wine for a complete dining experience. Buon appetito!

Lemon Sorbetto

Ingredients:

- 1 cup water
- 1 cup granulated sugar
- 1 cup freshly squeezed lemon juice (about 4-6 lemons)
- Zest of 1-2 lemons (optional, for extra flavor)
- 1/2 cup cold water

Instructions:

1. **Prepare Simple Syrup:**
    - In a small saucepan, combine 1 cup of water and 1 cup of granulated sugar. Heat over medium heat, stirring occasionally, until the sugar completely dissolves and the mixture comes to a simmer. Remove from heat and let it cool to room temperature.Cioppino
2. **Make the Sorbetto Base:**
    - In a large bowl, combine the freshly squeezed lemon juice and the cooled simple syrup. If using lemon zest, add it to the mixture for extra citrus flavor.
    - Stir in 1/2 cup of cold water to thin the mixture slightly.
3. **Chill the Mixture:**
    - Cover the bowl with plastic wrap and refrigerate the lemon mixture for at least 2-3 hours, or until thoroughly chilled.
4. **Churn the Sorbetto:**
    - Pour the chilled lemon mixture into your ice cream maker and churn according to the manufacturer's instructions. Churning usually takes about 20-30 minutes, or until the sorbetto reaches a smooth and creamy consistency.
5. **Freeze the Sorbetto:**
    - Transfer the churned sorbetto into a freezer-safe container. Smooth the top with a spatula, then cover with a lid or plastic wrap directly touching the surface of the sorbetto to prevent ice crystals from forming.
    - Freeze the sorbetto for at least 4 hours, or until firm.
6. **Serve:**
    - Before serving, let the sorbetto sit at room temperature for a few minutes to soften slightly for easier scooping.
    - Scoop the lemon sorbetto into bowls or serving glasses.
    - Garnish with a slice of lemon or fresh mint leaves, if desired.

Enjoy this homemade lemon sorbetto as a refreshing dessert on its own, or use it to cleanse the palate between courses during a meal. It's a delightful way to enjoy the bright and tangy flavors of fresh lemons in a cool and icy treat. Buon appetito!

Cioppino

Ingredients:

- 1/4 cup olive oil
- 1 onion, finely chopped
- 4 cloves garlic, minced
- 1 fennel bulb, thinly sliced
- 1 red bell pepper, diced
- 1/2 teaspoon red pepper flakes (adjust to taste)
- 1/2 cup white wine
- 1 can (28 ounces) crushed tomatoes
- 2 cups fish or seafood broth
- 1 bay leaf
- 1 teaspoon dried oregano
- 1 teaspoon dried basil
- Salt and freshly ground black pepper, to taste
- 1 pound firm white fish fillets (such as cod, halibut, or sea bass), cut into chunks
- 1 pound shellfish (such as clams, mussels, or shrimp), cleaned and scrubbed
- 1 pound crab legs or cooked crab meat
- Fresh parsley, chopped, for garnish
- Crusty bread, for serving

Instructions:

1. **Prepare the Base:**
    - In a large pot or Dutch oven, heat the olive oil over medium heat. Add the chopped onion, minced garlic, sliced fennel, diced red bell pepper, and red pepper flakes. Cook, stirring occasionally, until the vegetables are softened, about 5-7 minutes.
2. **Add Liquids and Seasonings:**
    - Pour in the white wine and cook for 2-3 minutes, allowing the alcohol to evaporate.
    - Add the crushed tomatoes, fish or seafood broth, bay leaf, dried oregano, and dried basil. Season with salt and black pepper to taste. Bring the mixture to a simmer.
3. **Cook the Seafood:**
    - Once the broth is simmering, add the chunks of white fish fillets, shellfish (clams and mussels), and crab legs (if using). Cover the pot and cook for about 5-7 minutes, or until the shellfish have opened and the fish is cooked through. Discard any unopened shellfish.
4. **Finish and Serve:**
    - Remove the bay leaf from the stew. Taste and adjust seasoning if needed.
    - Ladle the Cioppino into serving bowls, making sure to distribute the seafood evenly.

- - Garnish with chopped fresh parsley.
  - Serve hot with crusty bread on the side for dipping into the flavorful broth.

Cioppino is a delicious and comforting seafood stew that is perfect for special occasions or gatherings. It's best enjoyed with a group of friends or family, accompanied by a glass of white wine. Serve this hearty dish as a main course and savor the flavors of the sea in every spoonful. Buon appetito!

Cacio e Pepe

Ingredients:

- 1 pound (about 450g) spaghetti or bucatini pasta
- 1 1/2 cups grated Pecorino Romano cheese
- 1 tablespoon freshly cracked black pepper (adjust to taste)
- Salt, to taste
- Extra virgin olive oil (optional)

Instructions:

1. **Cook the Pasta:**
   - Bring a large pot of salted water to a boil. Add the spaghetti or bucatini pasta and cook according to the package instructions until al dente.
2. **Prepare the Sauce:**
   - While the pasta is cooking, in a large skillet or saucepan, toast the freshly cracked black pepper over medium heat for about 1 minute, until fragrant. Remove from heat.
3. **Combine Pasta and Sauce:**
   - Reserve about 1 cup of pasta cooking water, then drain the cooked pasta.
   - Immediately transfer the hot pasta to the skillet with the toasted pepper.
   - Gradually add the grated Pecorino Romano cheese to the pasta, tossing and stirring vigorously with tongs or a pasta fork. Add a splash of pasta cooking water as needed to create a creamy sauce that coats the pasta evenly. The heat from the pasta and a bit of the starchy pasta water will help melt the cheese and create a silky sauce.
4. **Serve:**
   - Divide the Cacio e Pepe pasta among serving plates or bowls.
   - Garnish with additional freshly cracked black pepper and a drizzle of extra virgin olive oil, if desired.
   - Serve immediately while hot and enjoy the simple, delicious flavors of this classic Roman dish!

Cacio e Pepe is best enjoyed fresh and hot, allowing the creamy cheese and peppery flavors to shine. It's a perfect dish for pasta lovers looking to experience authentic Italian cuisine with minimal ingredients. Buon appetito!

Pistachio Gelato

Ingredients:

- 1 cup shelled pistachio nuts (unsalted)
- 2 cups whole milk
- 1 cup heavy cream
- 3/4 cup granulated sugar
- 4 large egg yolks
- 1 teaspoon pure vanilla extract
- Pinch of salt

Instructions:

1. **Prepare the Pistachio Paste:**
    - In a food processor or blender, pulse the pistachio nuts until finely ground into a paste. Add a tablespoon of milk if needed to help grind them into a smooth consistency. Set aside.
2. **Make the Gelato Base:**
    - In a medium saucepan, combine the whole milk, heavy cream, and sugar. Heat over medium heat, stirring occasionally, until the mixture reaches a simmer and the sugar has dissolved.
3. **Temper the Egg Yolks:**
    - In a separate bowl, whisk the egg yolks until smooth. Gradually add about 1/2 cup of the hot milk mixture to the egg yolks, whisking constantly. This step helps to temper the egg yolks and prevent them from curdling when added to the hot liquid.
4. **Combine and Cook:**
    - Pour the tempered egg yolks into the saucepan with the remaining milk mixture, whisking continuously.
    - Cook over medium heat, stirring constantly with a wooden spoon or heatproof spatula, until the mixture thickens slightly and coats the back of the spoon. This usually takes about 5-7 minutes. Do not let it boil.
5. **Add Pistachio Paste:**
    - Remove the saucepan from heat. Stir in the pistachio paste, vanilla extract, and a pinch of salt until well combined.
6. **Chill the Mixture:**
    - Pour the gelato base through a fine-mesh sieve into a clean bowl to remove any solids. Cover the bowl with plastic wrap, pressing it directly onto the surface of the mixture to prevent a skin from forming.
    - Refrigerate the mixture for at least 4 hours or overnight until thoroughly chilled.
7. **Churn the Gelato:**
    - Once chilled, pour the pistachio gelato base into an ice cream maker and churn according to the manufacturer's instructions until it reaches a soft-serve consistency.

8. **Freeze the Gelato:**
    - Transfer the churned gelato into a freezer-safe container. Smooth the top with a spatula, then cover with a lid or plastic wrap directly touching the surface of the gelato to prevent ice crystals from forming.
    - Freeze the pistachio gelato for at least 4 hours, or until firm.
9. **Serve:**
    - Remove the pistachio gelato from the freezer a few minutes before serving to soften slightly.
    - Scoop the gelato into bowls or cones.
    - Garnish with chopped pistachio nuts, if desired, and enjoy the creamy, nutty flavors of homemade pistachio gelato!

Pistachio gelato is a delightful treat that captures the essence of pistachio nuts in a smooth and creamy frozen dessert. It's perfect for enjoying on its own or alongside other Italian sweets. Buon appetito!

Farfalle al Salmone

Ingredients:

- 1 pound (about 450g) farfalle pasta (bowtie pasta)
- 1 pound (about 450g) salmon fillet, skin removed and cut into bite-sized pieces
- 2 tablespoons olive oil
- 2 cloves garlic, minced
- 1/2 cup dry white wine
- 1 cup heavy cream
- 1/2 cup grated Parmesan cheese
- Zest of 1 lemon
- 1/4 cup fresh dill, chopped (or 1 tablespoon dried dill)
- Salt and freshly ground black pepper, to taste
- Fresh parsley, chopped, for garnish
- Lemon wedges, for serving

Instructions:

1. **Cook the Farfalle Pasta:**
    - Bring a large pot of salted water to a boil. Cook the farfalle pasta according to the package instructions until al dente. Drain and set aside, reserving about 1 cup of pasta cooking water.
2. **Prepare the Salmon:**
    - In a large skillet, heat olive oil over medium-high heat. Add the minced garlic and sauté for about 1 minute until fragrant.
    - Add the salmon pieces to the skillet. Cook for 3-4 minutes, stirring occasionally, until the salmon is lightly browned and cooked through. Remove the salmon from the skillet and set aside.
3. **Make the Creamy Sauce:**
    - Deglaze the skillet with the dry white wine, scraping up any browned bits from the bottom of the pan.
    - Reduce the heat to medium-low. Pour in the heavy cream and stir gently to combine. Let the sauce simmer for 2-3 minutes until slightly thickened.
    - Stir in the grated Parmesan cheese until melted and smooth.
4. **Combine Pasta and Sauce:**
    - Add the cooked farfalle pasta to the skillet with the creamy sauce. Toss well to coat the pasta evenly with the sauce. If the sauce is too thick, add a splash of reserved pasta cooking water to reach your desired consistency.
    - Gently fold in the cooked salmon pieces, lemon zest, and chopped dill. Season with salt and freshly ground black pepper to taste.
5. **Serve:**
    - Divide Farfalle al Salmone among serving plates or bowls.
    - Garnish with chopped fresh parsley and serve with lemon wedges on the side for squeezing over the pasta.

- Enjoy this creamy and flavorful pasta dish with a glass of white wine for a complete meal!

Farfalle al Salmone is a comforting and elegant dish that combines the richness of salmon with a creamy Parmesan sauce and bright hints of lemon and dill. It's perfect for a special dinner at home or for entertaining guests. Buon appetito!

Crostini ai Funghi

Ingredients:

- 1 French baguette, sliced into 1/2-inch thick rounds
- 1/4 cup olive oil, plus extra for drizzling
- 1 pound mixed mushrooms (such as cremini, shiitake, and oyster), finely chopped
- 2 cloves garlic, minced
- 1/4 cup dry white wine
- 1/4 cup heavy cream
- Salt and freshly ground black pepper, to taste
- 1 tablespoon fresh thyme leaves
- Grated Parmesan cheese, for garnish (optional)
- Fresh parsley, chopped, for garnish

Instructions:

1. **Prepare the Crostini:**
   - Preheat the oven to 400°F (200°C).
   - Place the baguette slices on a baking sheet. Brush both sides of each slice with olive oil. Bake in the preheated oven for about 8-10 minutes, flipping halfway through, until the crostini are golden and crispy. Remove from the oven and set aside.
2. **Cook the Mushrooms:**
   - In a large skillet, heat 1/4 cup of olive oil over medium heat. Add the minced garlic and cook for about 1 minute until fragrant.
   - Add the chopped mushrooms to the skillet. Cook, stirring occasionally, until the mushrooms are softened and lightly browned, about 5-7 minutes.
3. **Add Wine and Cream:**
   - Pour in the dry white wine, stirring to deglaze the skillet and scrape up any browned bits from the bottom. Cook for 2-3 minutes until the wine has reduced slightly.
   - Stir in the heavy cream and cook for another 2-3 minutes until the sauce thickens slightly. Season with salt and freshly ground black pepper to taste.
   - Remove the skillet from heat and stir in fresh thyme leaves.
4. **Assemble the Crostini:**
   - Spoon a generous amount of the mushroom mixture onto each crostini slice.
   - If desired, sprinkle grated Parmesan cheese over the tops of the crostini.
   - Drizzle with a little extra olive oil and garnish with chopped fresh parsley.
5. **Serve:**
   - Arrange the Crostini ai Funghi on a serving platter.
   - Serve immediately while warm, and enjoy this delicious appetizer with friends and family!

Crostini ai Funghi is a perfect starter for any Italian-inspired meal or as part of a cocktail party spread. The earthy mushrooms combined with garlic, wine, and cream create a rich and flavorful topping that pairs beautifully with crispy toasted bread. Buon appetito!

Tortellini in Brodo

Ingredients:

- 1 pound (about 450g) fresh tortellini (cheese-filled or meat-filled)
- 8 cups chicken broth (homemade or low-sodium store-bought)
- 2 carrots, peeled and diced
- 2 celery stalks, diced
- 1 small onion, diced
- 2 cloves garlic, minced
- 1 tablespoon olive oil
- Salt and freshly ground black pepper, to taste
- Fresh parsley, chopped, for garnish
- Grated Parmesan cheese, for serving (optional)

Instructions:

1. **Prepare the Vegetables:**
   - In a large pot or Dutch oven, heat olive oil over medium heat. Add diced carrots, celery, onion, and minced garlic. Sauté for about 5 minutes until vegetables are softened.
2. **Simmer the Broth:**
   - Pour in the chicken broth and bring the mixture to a boil. Reduce heat to low and let it simmer for about 15-20 minutes, allowing the flavors to meld together. Season with salt and pepper to taste.
3. **Cook the Tortellini:**
   - While the broth is simmering, cook the tortellini according to the package instructions in a separate pot of boiling salted water until they float to the top and are tender. Drain the tortellini and set aside.
4. **Combine Tortellini and Broth:**
   - Add the cooked tortellini to the simmering broth. Stir gently to combine and let them heat through for a couple of minutes.
5. **Serve:**
   - Ladle the Tortellini in Brodo into serving bowls, making sure to distribute tortellini and vegetables evenly.
   - Garnish with chopped fresh parsley and grated Parmesan cheese, if desired.
   - Serve hot as a comforting and satisfying soup.

Tortellini in Brodo is a versatile dish that can be adapted with different types of tortellini fillings and variations in the broth. It's a beloved Italian classic that highlights the simplicity of fresh pasta and a flavorful broth. Enjoy this dish as a starter or a light main course with a side of crusty bread. Buon appetito!

Bistecca alla Fiorentina

Ingredients:

- 1 or 2 Porterhouse steaks (about 1 1/2 to 2 inches thick), ideally from Chianina or another high-quality beef
- Salt, preferably coarse sea salt
- Freshly ground black pepper
- Extra virgin olive oil
- Optional: Rosemary sprigs and garlic cloves for additional flavor

Instructions:

1. **Prepare the Steak:**
   - Remove the steak(s) from the refrigerator about 30 minutes before cooking to bring them to room temperature. This allows for more even cooking.
2. **Season the Steak:**
   - Pat the steaks dry with paper towels to remove any excess moisture. Season both sides generously with coarse sea salt and freshly ground black pepper. Press the seasoning into the meat.
3. **Grill or Pan-Sear the Steak:**
   - Preheat your grill or a heavy-bottomed skillet (cast iron works well) over high heat until very hot.
   - Brush both sides of the steak lightly with olive oil.
   - If grilling: Place the steak directly over the hottest part of the grill. For a thick steak, grill for about 5-6 minutes per side for medium-rare, or adjust cooking time according to your desired doneness.
   - If pan-searing: Add a little olive oil to the hot skillet. Place the steak in the skillet and sear without moving for about 3-4 minutes per side for medium-rare, or adjust cooking time as needed.
4. **Rest the Steak:**
   - Once cooked to your liking, transfer the steak to a cutting board or platter and let it rest for 5-10 minutes. This allows the juices to redistribute and ensures a tender steak.
5. **Serve:**
   - Optionally, while resting, you can drizzle a little more olive oil over the steak and add a few sprigs of rosemary and garlic cloves to infuse extra flavor.
   - Slice the steak against the grain into thick slices.
   - Serve immediately, traditionally with a side of Tuscan bread (pane sciocco) to soak up the delicious juices.

"Bistecca alla Fiorentina" celebrates the natural flavors of high-quality beef with minimal seasoning, allowing the meat to shine. It's a beloved dish in Tuscany, especially when paired with a robust red wine like Chianti. Enjoy this rustic and flavorful steak as a centerpiece to a memorable meal. Buon appetito!

Pesto Genovese

Ingredients:

- 2 cups fresh basil leaves, packed
- 1/2 cup grated Parmesan cheese
- 1/2 cup extra virgin olive oil
- 1/3 cup pine nuts (you can also use walnuts for a variation)
- 2 cloves garlic, peeled
- Salt, to taste
- Freshly ground black pepper, to taste

Instructions:

1. **Toast the Pine Nuts (Optional):**
   - If desired, toast the pine nuts in a dry skillet over medium heat for a few minutes until lightly golden and fragrant. Stir frequently to prevent burning. Remove from heat and let them cool slightly.
2. **Prepare the Pesto:**
   - In a food processor or blender, combine the basil leaves, toasted pine nuts (or walnuts), grated Parmesan cheese, and peeled garlic cloves.
   - Pulse several times until the ingredients are finely chopped and blended.
3. **Add Olive Oil:**
   - With the food processor or blender running, gradually pour in the extra virgin olive oil in a steady stream. Continue blending until the mixture is smooth and well combined. You may need to stop and scrape down the sides of the bowl with a spatula as needed.
4. **Season to Taste:**
   - Taste the pesto and season with salt and freshly ground black pepper, adjusting to your preference.
5. **Serve or Store:**
   - Use the Pesto Genovese immediately as a sauce for pasta, as a spread on sandwiches or bruschetta, or as a topping for grilled meats and vegetables.
   - If storing, transfer the pesto to an airtight container and drizzle a little extra olive oil over the top to prevent oxidation. It can be stored in the refrigerator for up to a week or frozen for longer storage.

Tips:

- **Variations:** For a twist, you can substitute some or all of the basil with other herbs like parsley or mint, or use a combination of nuts such as walnuts or almonds.
- **Cooking with Pesto:** When using Pesto Genovese with pasta, reserve some pasta cooking water. Toss the drained pasta with pesto and a little pasta water to create a creamy sauce that coats the pasta evenly.

Pesto Genovese is a versatile and flavorful sauce that adds a taste of Italy to a wide range of dishes. Its fresh, herbaceous profile makes it a favorite in Italian cuisine and a delightful addition to your culinary repertoire. Buon appetito!

Zeppole di San Giuseppe

Ingredients:

For the Pastry:

- 1 cup water
- 1/2 cup unsalted butter
- Pinch of salt
- 1 cup all-purpose flour
- 4 large eggs

For the Custard Filling:

- 2 cups whole milk
- 4 large egg yolks
- 1/2 cup granulated sugar
- 1/4 cup cornstarch
- 1 teaspoon vanilla extract
- Lemon zest (optional)

For Frying and Topping:

- Vegetable oil, for frying
- Powdered sugar, for dusting
- Maraschino cherries or candied cherries, for garnish

Instructions:

1. **Make the Custard Filling:**
    - In a saucepan, heat the milk over medium heat until it just starts to simmer. Remove from heat.
    - In a separate bowl, whisk together the egg yolks, granulated sugar, and cornstarch until smooth and pale.
    - Gradually whisk the hot milk into the egg mixture, a little at a time, to temper the eggs.
    - Pour the mixture back into the saucepan and return to medium heat. Cook, stirring constantly, until the custard thickens and coats the back of a spoon (about 5-7 minutes).
    - Remove from heat and stir in the vanilla extract and lemon zest (if using). Transfer the custard to a bowl, cover with plastic wrap (directly on the surface to prevent a skin from forming), and chill in the refrigerator until cold.
2. **Prepare the Pastry Dough:**
    - In a medium saucepan, combine the water, butter, and salt. Bring to a boil over medium-high heat.

- Reduce the heat to low and add the flour all at once. Stir vigorously with a wooden spoon until the mixture forms a ball and pulls away from the sides of the pan (about 1-2 minutes). Remove from heat.
- Transfer the dough to a mixing bowl and let it cool slightly (about 5 minutes).

3. **Add Eggs:**
   - Add the eggs, one at a time, to the dough, beating well after each addition. The dough should be smooth and shiny.

4. **Fry the Zeppole:**
   - In a large, heavy-bottomed pot, heat vegetable oil to 350°F (175°C).
   - Drop spoonfuls of dough into the hot oil, using a second spoon to push the dough off the first spoon. Alternatively, you can pipe the dough into small rings directly into the oil.
   - Fry the zeppole in batches until golden brown and crispy, turning occasionally, about 3-4 minutes per batch.
   - Remove with a slotted spoon and drain on paper towels. Allow them to cool slightly.

5. **Assemble the Zeppole di San Giuseppe:**
   - Fill a pastry bag fitted with a round tip with the chilled custard.
   - Insert the tip into the side of each zeppole and gently squeeze to fill with custard. Alternatively, you can slice the zeppole horizontally and fill them like sandwiches.
   - Dust the filled zeppole generously with powdered sugar.
   - Garnish the top of each zeppole with a maraschino cherry or a piece of candied cherry.

6. **Serve:**
   - Zeppole di San Giuseppe are best served fresh. Enjoy them as a delicious treat on St. Joseph's Day or any special occasion!

These Zeppole di San Giuseppe are a delightful indulgence, combining crispy fried dough with creamy custard filling and a touch of sweetness. They are a beloved tradition in Italian cuisine and perfect for celebrating special days with family and friends. Buon appetito!

Pasta Primavera

Ingredients:

- 12 ounces (340g) pasta (such as fettuccine, linguine, or penne)
- 2 tablespoons olive oil
- 2 cloves garlic, minced
- 1 small onion, thinly sliced
- 1 red bell pepper, thinly sliced
- 1 yellow bell pepper, thinly sliced
- 1 medium zucchini, halved lengthwise and thinly sliced
- 1 cup cherry tomatoes, halved
- 1 cup broccoli florets
- 1 cup asparagus, cut into 1-inch pieces
- Salt and freshly ground black pepper, to taste
- 1/2 cup grated Parmesan cheese, plus extra for serving
- Fresh basil or parsley, chopped, for garnish

For the Sauce:

- 1/2 cup vegetable or chicken broth
- 1/2 cup heavy cream or half-and-half (optional for a creamier sauce)
- Zest and juice of 1 lemon
- 1/4 teaspoon red pepper flakes (optional)
- Salt and freshly ground black pepper, to taste

Instructions:

1. **Cook the Pasta:**
   - Bring a large pot of salted water to a boil. Cook the pasta according to the package instructions until al dente. Reserve 1 cup of pasta cooking water, then drain the pasta and set aside.
2. **Prepare the Vegetables:**
   - In a large skillet or pan, heat olive oil over medium heat. Add minced garlic and sliced onion. Cook for 2-3 minutes until fragrant and onions are translucent.
3. **Add Vegetables:**
   - Add sliced red and yellow bell peppers, zucchini, cherry tomatoes, broccoli florets, and asparagus to the skillet. Season with salt and black pepper. Cook, stirring occasionally, for about 5-7 minutes until the vegetables are tender-crisp.
4. **Make the Sauce:**
   - Pour vegetable or chicken broth into the skillet with the cooked vegetables. Add heavy cream or half-and-half (if using), lemon zest, lemon juice, and red pepper flakes (if using). Stir to combine and simmer for 2-3 minutes until heated through and slightly thickened. Adjust seasoning with salt and black pepper.
5. **Combine Pasta and Sauce:**

- Add the cooked pasta to the skillet with the vegetables and sauce. Toss gently to combine, adding reserved pasta cooking water as needed to loosen the sauce and coat the pasta evenly.
6. **Finish and Serve:**
    - Stir in grated Parmesan cheese until melted and incorporated into the sauce.
    - Remove from heat and garnish with chopped fresh basil or parsley.
    - Serve Pasta Primavera immediately, with extra grated Parmesan cheese on the side if desired.

Pasta Primavera is a delightful and versatile dish that showcases the bounty of spring vegetables. It's perfect for a light and flavorful meal, whether as a main course or a side dish. Enjoy the vibrant colors and fresh flavors of this classic Italian pasta dish! Buon appetito!

Sformato di Carciofi

Ingredients:

- 4-5 medium artichokes
- Juice of 1 lemon
- 2 tablespoons unsalted butter
- 2 tablespoons all-purpose flour
- 1 cup whole milk
- 3 large eggs, separated
- 1/2 cup grated Parmesan cheese
- Salt and freshly ground black pepper, to taste
- Pinch of nutmeg
- Butter or oil, for greasing

Instructions:

1. **Prepare the Artichokes:**
   - Fill a large bowl with water and add the lemon juice.
   - Trim the artichokes by removing tough outer leaves and trimming the tops. Cut off the stem and peel the remaining stem, then quarter the artichokes lengthwise and remove the fuzzy choke with a spoon.
   - Place the prepared artichokes in the lemon water to prevent browning.
2. **Cook the Artichokes:**
   - Bring a pot of salted water to a boil. Add the artichokes and cook until tender, about 15-20 minutes. Drain and let cool slightly, then chop into small pieces.
3. **Make the Custard:**
   - Preheat the oven to 350°F (175°C). Grease a 9-inch round baking dish or individual ramekins with butter or oil.
   - In a saucepan, melt the butter over medium heat. Stir in the flour and cook for 1-2 minutes until smooth and bubbly.
   - Gradually whisk in the milk, stirring constantly, until smooth and thickened.
   - Remove from heat and stir in the egg yolks, one at a time. Stir in the Parmesan cheese, chopped artichokes, salt, pepper, and nutmeg. Mix well.
4. **Whip the Egg Whites:**
   - In a clean bowl, beat the egg whites with a pinch of salt until stiff peaks form.
5. **Fold and Bake:**
   - Gently fold the whipped egg whites into the artichoke mixture until just combined.
   - Pour the mixture into the prepared baking dish or ramekins.
6. **Bake:**
   - Place the baking dish or ramekins in a larger baking pan. Pour hot water into the larger pan to create a water bath (about halfway up the sides of the baking dish).
   - Bake in the preheated oven for 35-40 minutes (less for individual ramekins), or until the top is golden brown and the center is set.
7. **Serve:**

- - Remove from the oven and let cool slightly before serving.
  - Sformato di Carciofi can be served warm or at room temperature. Garnish with additional grated Parmesan cheese and chopped parsley if desired.

Sformato di Carciofi is a wonderful dish that highlights the delicate flavor of artichokes in a creamy, custard-like texture. It's perfect for special occasions or as a unique addition to a dinner party menu. Enjoy the rich flavors of this Italian delight! Buon appetito!

Pollo alla Cacciatora

Ingredients:

- 4-6 chicken thighs or drumsticks, skin-on and bone-in
- Salt and freshly ground black pepper, to taste
- 2 tablespoons olive oil
- 1 onion, chopped
- 2 cloves garlic, minced
- 1 red bell pepper, sliced
- 1 yellow bell pepper, sliced
- 1/2 cup white or red wine
- 1 can (14 oz) diced tomatoes, with juices
- 1/2 cup chicken broth
- 1 teaspoon dried oregano
- 1 teaspoon dried thyme
- 1 teaspoon dried rosemary
- 1 bay leaf
- 1/4 cup chopped fresh parsley, for garnish
- Optional: 1/2 cup sliced mushrooms, black olives, or capers

Instructions:

1. **Season and Brown the Chicken:**
   - Season the chicken pieces with salt and pepper on both sides.
   - In a large skillet or Dutch oven, heat olive oil over medium-high heat. Add the chicken pieces, skin side down, and brown them on both sides until golden. Remove the chicken from the skillet and set aside.
2. **Saute the Aromatics:**
   - In the same skillet, add chopped onion and sauté for 3-4 minutes until softened.
   - Add minced garlic, sliced bell peppers, and any optional mushrooms, olives, or capers. Cook for another 3-4 minutes until vegetables are tender.
3. **Deglaze and Simmer:**
   - Pour in the wine and deglaze the skillet, scraping up any browned bits from the bottom.
   - Stir in the diced tomatoes with their juices, chicken broth, dried oregano, thyme, rosemary, and bay leaf. Bring to a simmer.
4. **Return Chicken to the Skillet:**
   - Return the browned chicken pieces to the skillet, nestling them into the sauce.
   - Cover the skillet with a lid and simmer gently over medium-low heat for about 30-35 minutes, or until the chicken is cooked through and tender. Stir occasionally.
5. **Finish and Serve:**
   - Taste and adjust seasoning with salt and pepper if needed.
   - Discard the bay leaf before serving.

- Garnish with chopped fresh parsley before serving.
6. **Serve:**
    - Serve Pollo alla Cacciatora hot, with the sauce spooned over the chicken pieces.
    - Optionally, serve over cooked pasta or rice, or with crusty bread to soak up the delicious sauce.

Pollo alla Cacciatora is a comforting and satisfying dish that brings together the flavors of tender chicken, savory tomatoes, and aromatic herbs. It's a perfect choice for a cozy family dinner or a gathering with friends. Buon appetito!

Zabaione

Ingredients:

- 4 large egg yolks
- 1/4 cup granulated sugar
- 1/2 cup sweet Marsala wine (traditionally used, but you can also use other sweet wines like Moscato or Madeira)
- Fresh berries or biscotti, for serving (optional)

Instructions:

1. **Prepare a Double Boiler:**
    - Fill a saucepan with a couple of inches of water and bring it to a simmer over medium heat. Reduce the heat to low to maintain a gentle simmer.
2. **Whisk Egg Yolks and Sugar:**
    - In a heatproof bowl (preferably stainless steel or glass), whisk together the egg yolks and sugar until well combined and slightly thickened.
3. **Cook the Zabaione:**
    - Place the bowl with the egg yolk mixture over the simmering water (the bottom of the bowl should not touch the water).
    - Gradually add the Marsala wine to the egg yolks, whisking constantly.
4. **Whisk Constantly:**
    - Continue whisking the mixture constantly but gently, ensuring the water underneath does not boil vigorously, for about 8-10 minutes or until the mixture thickens and triples in volume. It should be pale yellow and creamy.
5. **Serve:**
    - Remove the bowl from the heat and immediately divide the Zabaione into serving glasses or bowls.
    - Serve warm, or refrigerate for at least 1 hour to serve chilled.
    - Optionally, garnish with fresh berries or serve with biscotti on the side.

Tips:

- **Consistency:** The key to a good Zabaione is to whisk continuously and gently over low heat. The mixture should thicken gradually without curdling.
- **Wine Substitute:** If you prefer not to use alcohol, you can substitute the wine with an equal amount of fruit juice (such as apple or grape) mixed with a little lemon juice for acidity.

Zabaione is a delightful dessert that balances rich egg yolks with the sweetness of wine, creating a creamy and elegant treat. It's perfect for special occasions or as a finishing touch to a memorable Italian meal. Enjoy the velvety texture and nuanced flavors of homemade Zabaione!

Insalata di Mare

Ingredients:

- 1/2 pound (225g) mixed seafood (shrimp, calamari, mussels, octopus, etc.), cooked and cooled
- 1/2 red onion, thinly sliced
- 1 celery stalk, finely chopped
- 1/2 red bell pepper, diced
- 1/4 cup black olives, sliced
- 1/4 cup cherry tomatoes, halved
- 2 tablespoons fresh parsley, chopped
- Salt and freshly ground black pepper, to taste
- Juice of 1 lemon
- 3 tablespoons extra virgin olive oil

Instructions:

1. **Prepare the Seafood:**
    - If using fresh seafood, cook each type separately in boiling water until just cooked through. For shrimp and calamari, this usually takes 1-2 minutes. For octopus and mussels, follow specific cooking times until tender.
    - Rinse cooked seafood under cold water to stop cooking. Drain and let cool completely.
2. **Combine Ingredients:**
    - In a large bowl, combine the cooled seafood with sliced red onion, chopped celery, diced red bell pepper, sliced black olives, halved cherry tomatoes, and chopped fresh parsley.
3. **Make the Dressing:**
    - In a small bowl, whisk together the lemon juice and extra virgin olive oil. Season with salt and pepper to taste.
4. **Mix and Chill:**
    - Pour the dressing over the seafood and vegetable mixture. Gently toss to combine, ensuring all ingredients are coated with the dressing.
    - Cover the bowl and refrigerate for at least 30 minutes to allow flavors to meld.
5. **Serve:**
    - Serve Insalata di Mare chilled or at room temperature.
    - Optionally, garnish with additional chopped parsley before serving.

Tips:

- **Seafood Selection:** You can customize Insalata di Mare based on your preferences and availability of seafood. Use a combination of your favorite seafood, ensuring they are cooked properly and cooled before mixing.

- **Make Ahead:** This salad can be made a few hours in advance and kept refrigerated until ready to serve, making it a convenient option for entertaining.

Insalata di Mare is a versatile dish that can be served as an appetizer, side dish, or even a light main course. It's light, refreshing, and showcases the wonderful flavors of fresh seafood with a zesty dressing. Enjoy this Italian seafood salad as a delightful addition to your next meal! Buon appetito!

Stracciatella Soup

Ingredients:

- 6 cups chicken broth (homemade or store-bought)
- 2 cups fresh spinach leaves, chopped
- 2 large eggs
- 1/4 cup grated Parmesan cheese, plus extra for serving
- Salt and freshly ground black pepper, to taste
- Fresh parsley, chopped, for garnish (optional)

Instructions:

1. **Prepare the Broth:**
    - In a large pot, bring the chicken broth to a simmer over medium heat.
2. **Add Spinach:**
    - Add the chopped spinach to the simmering broth. Cook for about 2-3 minutes until the spinach wilts.
3. **Prepare the Egg Mixture:**
    - In a mixing bowl, whisk together the eggs, grated Parmesan cheese, salt, and pepper until well combined.
4. **Create Egg Ribbons:**
    - Once the spinach is wilted, reduce the heat to low. Slowly pour the egg mixture into the simmering broth in a thin stream, stirring gently with a fork or whisk in one direction.
    - The eggs will cook almost immediately, forming thin ribbons. Cook for another 1-2 minutes, stirring gently, until the egg ribbons are fully cooked.
5. **Adjust Seasoning and Serve:**
    - Taste the soup and adjust seasoning with salt and pepper if needed.
    - Ladle the Stracciatella Soup into serving bowls.
    - Garnish with additional grated Parmesan cheese and chopped fresh parsley, if desired.

Tips:

- **Variations:** You can customize Stracciatella Soup by adding other ingredients such as shredded cooked chicken, diced tomatoes, or small pasta like orzo.
- **Serve Warm:** This soup is best served immediately while hot. It's perfect as a light starter or a comforting meal on its own.

Stracciatella Soup is a comforting and satisfying dish that's quick and easy to prepare. It's a wonderful way to enjoy the delicate flavors of Italian cuisine with minimal effort. Buon appetito!

Tagliatelle al Ragu

Ingredients:

- 12 ounces (340g) tagliatelle pasta (fresh or dried)
- 1 tablespoon olive oil
- 1 onion, finely chopped
- 2 cloves garlic, minced
- 1 carrot, finely chopped
- 1 celery stalk, finely chopped
- 1/2 pound (225g) ground beef and/or pork (or a mix)
- 1/2 cup dry red wine
- 1 can (14 oz) crushed tomatoes
- 1/2 cup beef or chicken broth
- 1 bay leaf
- 1 teaspoon dried oregano
- 1 teaspoon dried basil
- Salt and freshly ground black pepper, to taste
- Grated Parmesan cheese, for serving
- Fresh basil or parsley, chopped, for garnish (optional)

Instructions:

1. **Cook the Pasta:**
   - Bring a large pot of salted water to a boil. Cook the tagliatelle pasta according to the package instructions until al dente. Drain and set aside, reserving some pasta water.
2. **Prepare the Ragu Sauce:**
   - In a large skillet or Dutch oven, heat olive oil over medium heat.
   - Add finely chopped onion, minced garlic, chopped carrot, and chopped celery. Cook, stirring occasionally, until vegetables are softened and onions are translucent (about 5-7 minutes).
3. **Brown the Meat:**
   - Add the ground beef and/or pork to the skillet. Cook, breaking up the meat with a wooden spoon, until browned and cooked through.
4. **Deglaze and Simmer:**
   - Pour in the dry red wine and cook for 2-3 minutes, scraping up any browned bits from the bottom of the skillet.
   - Stir in the crushed tomatoes, beef or chicken broth, bay leaf, dried oregano, dried basil, salt, and pepper. Bring to a simmer.
5. **Simmer the Sauce:**
   - Reduce the heat to low and let the ragu sauce simmer gently for about 30-40 minutes, stirring occasionally, until the flavors meld and the sauce thickens. If it becomes too thick, add a little more broth or pasta water.
6. **Combine Pasta and Sauce:**

- Add the cooked tagliatelle pasta to the skillet with the ragu sauce. Toss gently to coat the pasta evenly with the sauce. If needed, add a splash of reserved pasta water to loosen the sauce.
7. **Serve:**
   - Serve Tagliatelle al Ragu hot, garnished with grated Parmesan cheese and chopped fresh basil or parsley, if desired.

Tips:

- **Pasta Consistency:** The pasta should be cooked al dente (firm to the bite) as it will continue to cook slightly when combined with the hot ragu sauce.
- **Make Ahead:** The ragu sauce can be made ahead of time and stored in the refrigerator for up to 3 days or frozen for longer storage. Reheat gently before tossing with freshly cooked pasta.

Tagliatelle al Ragu is a classic Italian comfort food dish that's perfect for family meals or entertaining guests. The combination of tender pasta and savory meat sauce makes it a favorite for pasta lovers everywhere. Buon appetito!

Biscotti di Prato

Ingredients:

- 2 cups (250g) all-purpose flour
- 1 cup (200g) granulated sugar
- 1 teaspoon baking powder
- Pinch of salt
- Zest of 1 lemon or orange (optional)
- 3 large eggs
- 1 teaspoon vanilla extract
- 1 cup (150g) whole almonds, lightly toasted
- Extra flour for dusting

Instructions:

1. **Preheat the Oven:**
    - Preheat your oven to 350°F (180°C). Line a baking sheet with parchment paper.
2. **Prepare the Dough:**
    - In a large mixing bowl, whisk together the flour, sugar, baking powder, salt, and lemon or orange zest (if using).
    - In a separate bowl, lightly beat the eggs with the vanilla extract.
3. **Combine Ingredients:**
    - Make a well in the center of the dry ingredients and pour in the beaten eggs. Mix with a wooden spoon or spatula until a dough starts to form.
    - Add the toasted almonds and continue to mix until the almonds are evenly distributed and the dough comes together. It will be sticky.
4. **Shape the Biscotti:**
    - Lightly dust your hands and work surface with flour. Divide the dough into two equal portions.
    - Shape each portion into a log about 12 inches (30 cm) long and 2 inches (5 cm) wide. Place the logs on the prepared baking sheet, leaving space between them as they will spread slightly during baking.
5. **First Bake:**
    - Bake the logs in the preheated oven for 25-30 minutes, or until they are lightly golden and firm to the touch.
6. **Cool and Slice:**
    - Remove the baking sheet from the oven and let the logs cool for about 10-15 minutes, or until they are cool enough to handle.
    - Reduce the oven temperature to 325°F (160°C).
    - Using a serrated knife, carefully slice the logs diagonally into 1/2-inch (1 cm) thick slices.
7. **Second Bake:**

- Arrange the biscotti cut-side down on the baking sheet. Bake for an additional 10-15 minutes, turning the biscotti halfway through baking, until they are golden and crisp.
- Transfer the biscotti to a wire rack to cool completely.
8. **Serve:**
    - Biscotti di Prato are traditionally served with Vin Santo for dipping. They can also be enjoyed on their own as a crunchy treat with coffee or tea.

Tips:

- **Toasting Almonds:** To toast almonds, spread them in a single layer on a baking sheet and bake in a preheated oven at 350°F (180°C) for 8-10 minutes, or until lightly golden and fragrant. Let cool before using in the recipe.
- **Storage:** Store cooled biscotti in an airtight container at room temperature for up to 2 weeks. They can also be frozen for longer storage.

Biscotti di Prato are a delightful Italian treat with a satisfying crunch and nutty flavor. They make a wonderful homemade gift and are perfect for enjoying any time of day. Enjoy baking and savoring these classic Italian biscotti!

Spiedini alla Romana

Ingredients:

- 1 pound (450g) pork tenderloin or veal, cut into 1-inch cubes
- 8 slices pancetta or thinly sliced prosciutto
- 1/4 cup extra virgin olive oil
- 2 cloves garlic, minced
- 2 tablespoons fresh parsley, finely chopped
- Zest of 1 lemon
- Salt and freshly ground black pepper, to taste
- Wooden skewers, soaked in water for at least 30 minutes (to prevent burning)

Instructions:

1. **Prepare the Marinade:**
   - In a bowl, whisk together the olive oil, minced garlic, chopped parsley, lemon zest, salt, and pepper.
2. **Assemble the Skewers:**
   - Preheat your grill or grill pan over medium-high heat.
   - Thread the marinated meat cubes onto the wooden skewers, alternating with pieces of pancetta or prosciutto. Fold the pancetta or prosciutto around the meat cubes as you skewer them.
3. **Grill the Skewers:**
   - Brush the assembled skewers with a little extra marinade.
   - Place the skewers on the preheated grill or grill pan. Grill for about 3-4 minutes per side, or until the meat is cooked through and nicely charred, and the pancetta or prosciutto is crisp.
4. **Serve:**
   - Remove the Spiedini alla Romana from the grill and let them rest for a few minutes.
   - Serve the skewers hot, optionally garnished with additional chopped parsley and lemon wedges.

Tips:

- **Variations:** You can also add cherry tomatoes, bell peppers, or onions to the skewers for additional flavor and color.
- **Oven Baking:** If you don't have a grill, you can bake the skewers in a preheated oven at 400°F (200°C) for about 15-20 minutes, turning once halfway through, until the meat is cooked through.

Spiedini alla Romana is a delicious and savory dish that highlights the simplicity and flavors of Italian cooking. It's perfect for a summer barbecue or as a main course served with a side of grilled vegetables or a fresh salad. Buon appetito!

Pasta all'Amatriciana

Ingredients:

- 12 ounces (340g) bucatini, spaghetti, or rigatoni pasta
- 1/4 pound (115g) guanciale or pancetta, diced
- 1 tablespoon extra virgin olive oil
- 1 small onion, finely chopped
- 2 cloves garlic, minced
- 1/4 teaspoon red pepper flakes (adjust to taste)
- 1 can (14 oz) crushed tomatoes
- 1/2 cup dry white wine (optional)
- Salt and freshly ground black pepper, to taste
- 1/2 cup grated Pecorino Romano cheese, plus extra for serving
- Fresh parsley or basil, chopped, for garnish (optional)

Instructions:

1. **Cook the Pasta:**
   - Bring a large pot of salted water to a boil. Cook the pasta according to package instructions until al dente. Reserve about 1 cup of pasta cooking water, then drain the pasta and set aside.
2. **Prepare the Sauce:**
   - In a large skillet or sauté pan, heat the olive oil over medium heat. Add the diced guanciale or pancetta and cook until crispy and golden brown, about 5-7 minutes.
3. **Saute Aromatics:**
   - Add the finely chopped onion to the skillet with the guanciale. Cook until the onion is soft and translucent, about 3-4 minutes.
   - Stir in the minced garlic and red pepper flakes, and cook for another 1-2 minutes until fragrant.
4. **Add Tomatoes and Wine:**
   - Pour in the crushed tomatoes and stir to combine. If using, add the dry white wine and simmer for about 10-15 minutes, allowing the flavors to meld and the sauce to thicken slightly.
   - Season with salt and black pepper to taste. Remember, guanciale and Pecorino Romano are salty, so adjust salt accordingly.
5. **Combine Pasta and Sauce:**
   - Add the cooked pasta to the skillet with the sauce. Toss gently to coat the pasta evenly with the sauce. If the sauce seems too thick, add a splash of reserved pasta cooking water to loosen it.
6. **Finish and Serve:**
   - Remove from heat and stir in the grated Pecorino Romano cheese.
   - Serve Pasta all'Amatriciana hot, garnished with extra grated cheese and chopped parsley or basil, if desired.

Tips:

- **Guanciale Substitute:** If guanciale is not available, pancetta is a good substitute. It won't be exactly the same, but it will still be delicious.
- **Wine Substitute:** If you prefer not to use wine, you can omit it. Just add a bit more pasta cooking water or broth to achieve the desired sauce consistency.
- **Variations:** Some variations include adding a splash of balsamic vinegar or using fresh tomatoes instead of canned.

Pasta all'Amatriciana is a flavorful and satisfying dish that showcases the essence of Italian cuisine. Enjoy this hearty pasta with a glass of red wine and crusty bread for a truly authentic experience. Buon appetito!

Polpo alla Griglia

Ingredients:

- 1 large octopus (about 2-3 pounds or 900g-1.4kg), cleaned
- 1/4 cup extra virgin olive oil
- 2 cloves garlic, minced
- Juice of 1 lemon
- 1 teaspoon dried oregano
- Salt and freshly ground black pepper, to taste
- Fresh parsley, chopped, for garnish
- Lemon wedges, for serving

Instructions:

1. **Prepare the Octopus:**
   - If your octopus is not already cleaned, rinse it under cold water and remove the beak, eyes, and internal organs.
   - Optional step: Tenderize the octopus by vigorously hitting it against a hard surface (like a cutting board) for a few minutes. This helps to break down the fibers and tenderize the meat.
2. **Pre-cook the Octopus:**
   - Bring a large pot of salted water to a boil. Add the octopus and reduce the heat to low. Simmer gently for about 45-60 minutes, or until the octopus is tender when pierced with a fork.
   - Note: Cooking time can vary depending on the size and thickness of the octopus. Check tenderness periodically.
3. **Marinate the Octopus:**
   - In a bowl, whisk together the extra virgin olive oil, minced garlic, lemon juice, dried oregano, salt, and pepper.
4. **Grill the Octopus:**
   - Preheat your grill to medium-high heat.
   - Remove the octopus from the pot and pat dry with paper towels. Brush the octopus with the marinade mixture, ensuring it is well coated.
   - Place the octopus directly on the grill grates. Grill for about 3-4 minutes per side, or until nicely charred and heated through.
5. **Serve:**
   - Transfer the grilled octopus to a serving platter. Sprinkle with chopped fresh parsley and serve with lemon wedges on the side.

Tips:

- **Tentacles:** If the octopus has long tentacles, you can curl them up on skewers or fold them to fit better on the grill.

- **Charring:** Don't be afraid to char the octopus slightly—it adds flavor and enhances the appearance of the dish.
- **Presentation:** Serve Grilled Octopus as an appetizer or main dish, accompanied by a side salad, grilled vegetables, or crusty bread.

Grilled Octopus is a delightful dish that captures the essence of Mediterranean cuisine with its simplicity and bold flavors. Enjoy this tender and flavorful seafood dish with family and friends. Buon appetito!

Sfogliatelle

Ingredients:

For the Dough:

- 2 cups (250g) all-purpose flour, plus extra for dusting
- 1/4 teaspoon salt
- 1/2 cup (115g) unsalted butter, chilled and diced
- 1/2 cup (120ml) cold water

For the Filling:

- 1 pound (450g) ricotta cheese, drained
- 1/2 cup (100g) granulated sugar
- 1/2 cup (60g) semolina flour
- Zest of 1 lemon
- 1 teaspoon vanilla extract
- 1/4 teaspoon ground cinnamon (optional)
- 1/4 cup (60ml) whole milk (if needed to adjust consistency)

For Assembly:

- 1 cup (230g) unsalted butter, melted (for brushing layers)
- Powdered sugar, for dusting

Instructions:

1. **Prepare the Dough:**
    - In a large bowl, whisk together the flour and salt. Add the chilled diced butter and rub it into the flour using your fingertips until the mixture resembles coarse crumbs.
    - Gradually add the cold water, mixing with a fork or pastry cutter, until the dough comes together. Form the dough into a ball, cover with plastic wrap, and refrigerate for at least 30 minutes.
2. **Make the Filling:**
    - In a mixing bowl, combine the drained ricotta cheese, granulated sugar, semolina flour, lemon zest, vanilla extract, and ground cinnamon (if using). Mix until well combined and smooth. If the filling seems too thick, add a little whole milk to adjust the consistency. Cover and refrigerate until ready to use.
3. **Prepare the Layers:**
    - Preheat your oven to 400°F (200°C). Line a baking sheet with parchment paper.
    - Divide the dough into 4 equal portions. On a lightly floured surface, roll out one portion of dough into a very thin rectangle, almost transparent. Brush the dough with melted butter.

- Starting from the long side, roll the dough into a tight log. Cut the log into slices about 1 inch (2.5 cm) thick.
4. **Shape the Sfogliatelle:**
   - Take each slice and press down on the cut side with the palm of your hand to flatten slightly. Using your fingers, stretch and pull each slice gently to form a thin oval shape.
5. **Fill and Shape:**
   - Place a spoonful of the ricotta filling onto the center of each oval. Fold one side of the oval over the filling, then fold the other side over, overlapping slightly to form a shell-like shape.
   - Place the shaped sfogliatelle on the prepared baking sheet, seam side down.
6. **Bake:**
   - Brush the tops of the sfogliatelle with melted butter. Bake in the preheated oven for 20-25 minutes, or until golden brown and crisp.
7. **Serve:**
   - Remove from the oven and let cool slightly on a wire rack. Dust with powdered sugar before serving warm or at room temperature.

Tips:

- **Chilling Dough:** Chilling the dough helps relax the gluten and makes it easier to roll out thinly.
- **Handling Sfogliatelle:** Work quickly with the dough slices as they can dry out and become brittle. Keep them covered with a damp cloth while working.
- **Variations:** Sfogliatelle can also be filled with other fillings such as almond paste or pastry cream, depending on regional variations.

Sfogliatelle are a labor of love but well worth the effort for their crisp, flaky layers and creamy ricotta filling. They are a delightful treat for special occasions or as a sweet indulgence with coffee or tea. Enjoy the authentic taste of Naples with homemade sfogliatelle!

Zuppa di Pesce

Ingredients:

- 1 pound (450g) mixed seafood (such as shrimp, mussels, clams, squid, firm white fish like cod or halibut), cleaned and de-bearded if necessary
- 2 tablespoons extra virgin olive oil
- 1 onion, finely chopped
- 2 cloves garlic, minced
- 1 carrot, diced
- 1 celery stalk, diced
- 1 red bell pepper, diced
- 1/2 cup dry white wine
- 1 can (14 oz) crushed tomatoes
- 4 cups fish or seafood broth (homemade or store-bought)
- 1 bay leaf
- 1 teaspoon dried oregano
- Salt and freshly ground black pepper, to taste
- Fresh parsley, chopped, for garnish
- Crusty bread, for serving

Instructions:

1. **Prepare the Seafood:**
    - If using whole fish, fillet and cut into bite-sized pieces. Clean and devein shrimp. Scrub and debeard mussels and clams. Cut squid into rings or leave whole if small.
2. **Make the Soup Base:**
    - In a large pot or Dutch oven, heat the olive oil over medium heat. Add the chopped onion, garlic, carrot, celery, and red bell pepper. Cook, stirring occasionally, until the vegetables are softened, about 5-7 minutes.
3. **Add Wine and Tomatoes:**
    - Pour in the dry white wine and cook for 2-3 minutes, allowing the alcohol to evaporate.
    - Stir in the crushed tomatoes and cook for another 5 minutes, stirring occasionally.
4. **Simmer the Broth:**
    - Add the fish or seafood broth to the pot. Stir in the bay leaf, dried oregano, salt, and pepper. Bring the mixture to a simmer and let it cook for about 15-20 minutes to allow the flavors to meld.
5. **Add Seafood:**
    - Add the mixed seafood to the pot. Cook for 5-10 minutes, or until the seafood is cooked through. Be careful not to overcook the seafood, as it can become tough.
6. **Serve:**
    - Remove the bay leaf from the soup. Taste and adjust seasoning with salt and pepper if needed.

- - Ladle the Zuppa di Pesce into bowls. Garnish with chopped fresh parsley.
  - Serve hot, accompanied by crusty bread for dipping into the flavorful broth.

Tips:

- **Variations:** You can customize Zuppa di Pesce based on the seafood you prefer or what's available. Add scallops, lobster tail, or even octopus for variety.
- **Broth:** For a richer flavor, you can use a combination of fish and shrimp broth, or seafood stock.
- **Wine Substitute:** If you prefer not to use wine, you can skip it and add a splash of lemon juice for acidity.

Zuppa di Pesce is a comforting and satisfying dish that showcases the fresh flavors of the sea. It's perfect for a special dinner or as a warming meal on a chilly evening. Enjoy the taste of Italy with this delicious seafood soup!

Bresaola e Rucola

Ingredients:

- 4 ounces (about 100g) thinly sliced bresaola
- 2 cups fresh arugula (rucola), washed and dried
- 1/2 cup shaved Parmesan cheese
- Extra virgin olive oil
- Balsamic vinegar (optional)
- Salt and freshly ground black pepper, to taste

Instructions:

1. **Prepare the Ingredients:**
   - Arrange the thinly sliced bresaola on a serving platter or individual plates.
   - Wash and dry the fresh arugula thoroughly. Place the arugula on top of the bresaola.
2. **Assemble the Dish:**
   - Scatter the shaved Parmesan cheese over the arugula.
3. **Season and Dress:**
   - Drizzle the dish with extra virgin olive oil. If desired, add a touch of balsamic vinegar for extra flavor.
   - Season with salt and freshly ground black pepper to taste.
4. **Serve:**
   - Serve Bresaola e Rucola immediately as an appetizer or light meal.

Tips:

- **Variations:** You can add cherry tomatoes, slices of fresh figs, or even a squeeze of lemon juice to enhance the flavors.
- **Presentation:** Arrange the ingredients neatly on the plate for an appealing presentation.
- **Accompaniments:** Serve with crusty bread or grissini (breadsticks) on the side.

Bresaola e Rucola is a delightful dish that showcases the delicate flavors of bresaola paired with the peppery bite of arugula and the richness of Parmesan cheese. It's quick to assemble and perfect for any occasion where you want to enjoy a taste of Italian simplicity. Buon appetito!

Melanzane alla Parmigiana

Ingredients:

- 2 large eggplants, sliced into 1/2-inch rounds
- Salt, for sweating eggplant
- Olive oil, for frying
- 2 cups tomato sauce (homemade or store-bought)
- 1 cup grated Parmigiano-Reggiano cheese
- 8 oz fresh mozzarella cheese, sliced
- Fresh basil leaves, torn (optional)

For Tomato Sauce:

- 2 tablespoons olive oil
- 2 cloves garlic, minced
- 1 can (14 oz) crushed tomatoes
- Salt and pepper, to taste
- 1 teaspoon dried oregano
- 1/2 teaspoon red pepper flakes (optional)

Instructions:

1. **Prepare the Eggplant:**
    - Slice the eggplants into 1/2-inch rounds. Place the slices in a colander and sprinkle each layer with salt. Let them sit for about 30 minutes to draw out excess moisture and bitterness. Rinse the salt off and pat dry with paper towels.
2. **Fry the Eggplant:**
    - In a large skillet, heat olive oil over medium-high heat. Fry the eggplant slices in batches until golden brown on both sides, adding more oil as needed. Transfer the fried eggplant slices to a plate lined with paper towels to drain excess oil.
3. **Make the Tomato Sauce:**
    - In the same skillet used for frying (or a separate saucepan), heat 2 tablespoons of olive oil over medium heat. Add minced garlic and sauté until fragrant.
    - Pour in crushed tomatoes and season with salt, pepper, dried oregano, and red pepper flakes (if using). Simmer for about 10-15 minutes, stirring occasionally, until the sauce thickens slightly.
4. **Assemble the Dish:**
    - Preheat your oven to 375°F (190°C).
    - Spread a thin layer of tomato sauce on the bottom of a baking dish.
    - Arrange a layer of fried eggplant slices on top of the sauce. Spread a layer of tomato sauce over the eggplant slices, then sprinkle with grated Parmigiano-Reggiano cheese.
    - Add another layer of fried eggplant slices, followed by tomato sauce and Parmigiano-Reggiano cheese. Continue layering until all the eggplant slices are

used, finishing with a layer of tomato sauce and grated Parmigiano-Reggiano cheese on top.

5. **Add Mozzarella and Bake:**
   - Arrange sliced mozzarella cheese evenly over the top layer of tomato sauce and sprinkle with additional grated Parmigiano-Reggiano cheese if desired.
   - Bake in the preheated oven for 30-35 minutes, or until the cheese is melted and bubbly.
6. **Serve:**
   - Remove from the oven and let the Melanzane alla Parmigiana rest for a few minutes before serving.
   - Garnish with torn fresh basil leaves, if desired, and serve warm.

Tips:

- **Baking Dish:** Use a baking dish that's large enough to fit all the layers comfortably, about 9x13 inches.
- **Make Ahead:** You can assemble the dish ahead of time and refrigerate it before baking. Just allow a few extra minutes of baking time if baking from chilled.
- **Variations:** Some recipes add a layer of ricotta cheese mixed with egg and herbs between the layers of eggplant for added richness.

Melanzane alla Parmigiana is a comforting and flavorful dish that pairs well with a side of crusty bread or a simple green salad. It's a wonderful way to enjoy the flavors of Italian cuisine with the richness of eggplant and cheese. Buon appetito!

Gelato Affogato

Ingredients:

- 1 scoop of vanilla gelato (or any flavor of your choice)
- 1 shot of freshly brewed espresso (about 1-2 ounces)

Instructions:

1. **Brew the Espresso:**
   - Start by brewing a shot of espresso using an espresso machine. You can also use a stovetop espresso maker (Moka pot) or a strong brewed coffee if espresso is not available.
2. **Prepare the Gelato:**
   - Place a scoop of vanilla gelato (or your preferred gelato flavor) into a serving glass or bowl.
3. **Assemble the Gelato Affogato:**
   - Pour the freshly brewed hot espresso over the gelato scoop. The heat from the espresso will start to melt the gelato slightly, creating a creamy and flavorful dessert.
4. **Serve Immediately:**
   - Serve Gelato Affogato immediately while the espresso is hot and the gelato is cold and creamy.

Variations:

- **Alcoholic Affogato:** For a more indulgent treat, you can add a splash of your favorite liqueur such as amaretto, Frangelico, or Baileys Irish Cream to the espresso before pouring it over the gelato.
- **Flavor Variations:** Experiment with different gelato flavors such as chocolate, hazelnut, or pistachio to create unique combinations with the espresso.
- **Toppings:** Garnish with shaved chocolate, cocoa powder, or a sprinkle of nuts for added texture and flavor.

Gelato Affogato is a simple yet elegant dessert that balances the creamy sweetness of gelato with the rich, bold flavors of espresso. It's perfect for serving after a meal or as a refreshing treat any time of day. Enjoy the delightful taste of Italy with this easy-to-make dessert!

www.ingramcontent.com/pod-product-compliance
Lightning Source LLC
LaVergne TN
LVHW061945070526
838199LV00060B/3986